Finding the
Stillness Within
in a Busy World

Finding the Stillness Within in a Busy World

Sue Vaughan

SAFFRON WALDEN
THE C. W. DANIEL COMPANY LIMITED

First published in Great Britain in 1995
by The C. W. Daniel Company Limited
1 Church Path, Saffron Walden
Essex, CB10 1JP, England

ISBN 0 85207 283 X

Production in association with
Book Production Consultants plc, Cambridge

Typeset by KeyStar, St Ives, Cambridgeshire

Printed and bound by WSOY, Finland

**Dedicated to
Rhianon,
my friend,
my teacher,
my playmate
and
beautiful daughter.**

Contents

Acknowledgements

I would like to acknowledge the following people for their love and support whilst I was writing this book. Thank you, Rhianon, as always, you inspired me with your wisdom, humour and spirituality. Thanks, Karen, for all your practical help, for helping me to make friends with my computer and for always believing in me. Charlotte, your friendship feels like a warm blanket, thank-you for that. Thank you, Lindy, for always being there and being my big sister sometimes. Thank you to all my family especially my parents. I now know why I chose you all so thank you for having me. Jason, thanks for providing my computer even though in the early days I didn't appreciate what a wonderful tool it would turn out to be. Thank you to all the wonderful, courageous people that I have worked with in therapy and, of course, thankyou to all my friends seen and unseen.

The relaxation technique (Five Breaths) and the meditation (The Standing Stone) are reproduced in this book by kind permission of The National College of Hypnosis and Psychotherapy.

Introduction

In my work as a therapist, I have seen only too well how stress, anxiety, repressed or denied emotions, negative beliefs or a lack of self-esteem can affect the whole person; mind, body and spirit. These issues can stop us from receiving the love, success and joy that we truly deserve and that life can offer us if only we are willing to receive them. In this book, I offer a practical guide to deal with these issues and help you to find the inner peace that is your birthright.

Whether I work with someone in my capacity as a clinical nutritionist, a counsellor or workshop facilitator, I feel that the most important part of my job is to enable them to take responsibility for their physical and emotional well-being; helping them become more aware of the dynamics of their bodies and minds and then gently guiding them to choose the appropriate action.

In the past, many of us have given the responsibility for our happiness and well-being to our parents, partners or society. I have written this book to empower you with a 'tool box' of useful techniques, exercises and meditations that you can implement in your life to help you to live in a busy world with the knowledge that there is a nurturing stillness constantly there within you. You will find ways to clear away the clutter that is blocking your progress towards living a more fulfilled life, and others to allow you to let more love into your life.

Another factor in my desire to write this book is to take the mystique out of meditation; to show how it can be a part of everyday reality, however stressful, busy or dynamic your life may be. When you learn to surrender fully to the present moment, walking, washing the car or even cleaning the kitchen floor can be a meditation. (Honestly!)

Meditation needn't be something that is reserved for the hermits or yogis. It is not necessary to twist your body into impossible shapes and adhere to an ascetic lifestyle 'denying the flesh'. Those techniques are for the hermits and yogis but we can find that wonderful peace and serenity within ourselves in a much simpler and more graceful way that can blend beautifully with the razzmatazz of modern living.

Channelling various beings from the spirit world has become very fashionable in some New Age circles these days but I can't help thinking that channelling is not something special; for the elite few that are 'psychic'. I truly believe that each and every one of us has access to the most wonderful resources within ourselves; that wellspring of wisdom, our intuition. When our intuition, that still voice within, is refined and tuned into we can all become the most incredible 'channels' of creativity and spontaneous aliveness.

I have followed my intuition where it has led me; learned from many teachers and schools of thought. I have been inspired by the beauty of our world without ignoring its sorrows and apparent negativity. But probably the most valuable lessons that I have learned along my life path have been gleaned from finding the stillness within myself: through finding an awareness of my self-worth, healing the emotions I carried with me from my childhood, learning to trust and respect myself and realising that I truly do create my reality from within myself.

I have discovered the magic of the intricacies of our physical bodies from my studies in anatomy and clinical nutrition. I constantly marvel at the complexities of our unconscious minds and emotional memory through my work as a counsellor. I celebrate the excitement that I feel accepting the challenge of the adventure of life itself. The greatest miracle of all, however, is that in sensing, feeling and trusting that still voice within, I can recognize that same essence within others and I no longer feel separate. I realise that we are all, literally, one and the same under the skin.

Our lives can be so hectic, so crammed with concerns about our relationships, jobs or the lack of them, society's expectations and our own, that it is easy to lose track of who we are and what we are feeling. This book is written to help you to find that stillness in the whirlpool of life. It is a path which I tread to find peace within myself and for that reason it is one that I wish to share. This book is a journey to lead you to that place within you where you can create a positive future for yourself. A journey to lead you to being able to live more fully in your world, be true to yourself, enjoy satisfying relationships and have fun just being yourself.

The book is in five parts. Part One is devoted to clearing the debris that is preventing you from experiencing that inner peace that is your birthright. Part Two will show you many different ways of stilling and relaxing the mind and body. Part Three looks at how you can maintain that stillness in a busy world and Part Four will show you how you can allow love to flow more easily into your life. The fifth and final part of the journey looks at the interconnectedness of the human family, the 'I' that is 'We', and how our awareness of this can transform not only our environment but our world.

If you are one of those people who want to get to the last page quickly, are eager to know what it's all about, then read straight through and then again to work through the exercises, visualisations and techniques. If you are the more methodical type then work through the book as you go. Either way, thank you for joining me and let's start to find the stillness within together.

Part One: Clearing the Debris

1 Value and Appreciate Yourself

In Part One, we will be looking at ways of discovering and clearing the blocks, resistances and any negative beliefs that may be preventing you from finding that nurturing stillness within yourself.

So before you go any further with this book, I would like to suggest that you take a few moments out and do a very simple exercise.

Go up to the nearest mirror and look at your reflection. Don't be critical. It doesn't matter if your hair is out of place. Simply smile and acknowledge yourself. You can become your very best friend. Maybe you have not been very kind to yourself in the past. That's OK. You can make it up to yourself from now. Give yourself a saucy wink and a knowing smile and just say, 'Hi, (your name)'. If you feel silly, it's fine - maybe you have just met and you feel shy. If you feel like giving yourself the 'thumbs-up' sign feel free and when you are ready come back to the book.

Try this out often and even though it may feel uncomfortable at first, it is a very effective way of increasing your self-awareness and self-esteem. Try it in the morning to greet the 'new you' of the day. Usually we just look in mirrors to do our hair, shave, put on make-up or to give ourselves a hard time because of that spot that seems to be neon-lit, the hair that just won't do what it is supposed to or the figure that is not what we think it ought to be.

We know that no-one scrutinises us the way we scrutinise ourselves, so why do we do it? It's almost as if we don't demand perfection from anyone else but ourselves. Or is it that we just feel we are not quite good enough? Good enough for whom? Sometimes just tell your reflection that you are OK. The way you look, act and feel contribute to making you the person that you are. You don't need to be perfect, just be yourself. I am always puzzled when I occasionally have one of, what I call, my 'ugly days' just before my period. I look at my reflection and even though I know it is the same face that I approved of the day before, I don't feel happy with what I see. The only thing that is different is how I feel within. I really need to be gentle with myself on those days!

Another way of being good to ourselves as well as increasing our self-esteem is to allow positive feedback.

How do you cope with compliments? Do you accept them gracefully with a simple 'Thank you' and a smile or do you reject them as undeserved?

Although I don't think it is peculiar to this country, I think the British 'reserve', the self-effacing stiff upper lip that we have been brought up with, has a lot to answer for. It's almost seen as a virtue to put ourselves down, never to be seen to blow our own trumpets. So as not to seem big-headed or egotistical, we can often go completely the other way and put ourselves down.

I know that in the past if someone said to me, for example, "Your hair is looking nice today", I would cancel it out by saying something like, "Well, it ought to with the money I spend at the hairdressers!" Likewise, I would cancel out a compliment such as, "That was a job well done" by saying, "Not really, I could have done better." Sound familiar?

I remember when I decided that for one whole week I would accept all compliments with just 'Thankyou'. A nasty little voice within told me "Well you probably won't get any anyway." But I did and it was excruciating to accept the compliments that I received. I felt all sorts of resistances coming up, all kinds of reasons why they were saying it but not meaning it. "They are only saying that to be nice." What I realised was that deep down I felt that I didn't deserve the praise. I didn't somehow feel worthy. Accepting compliments as gracefully as I could was a good step towards finding an awareness of my self-worth.

Rejecting compliments out of hand is a bit like saying that you don't deserve to accept a beautiful gift that someone has chosen carefully and wrapped with love. We would not do that to someone, would we? Honest compliments are such positive feedback so allow yourself to feel deserving and feel good about yourself as a result. Accept the compliment gracefully; this will help the person who has complimented you to feel gratified for having done so, and allow yourself to receive the support that can be so valuable at times.

Try it out. Maybe just like I did. Commit yourself to a week of accepting compliments and flattery with a simple 'Thank you' and a smile. If you feel any resistances coming up, stay with them and look at them. You can learn from them. They will give you clues to where your negative beliefs about deservability are coming from.

In Chapter Four we will be looking at other ways to look up and edit those negative beliefs and reprogram for the wonderful future that you truly do deserve.

Of course, the other side of receiving compliments is to give them. We all know the warm glow that we feel when we have allowed ourselves to receive some positive feedback. It's good to be appreciated. It's also so good to give someone else that warm glow by honestly appreciating them. It sometimes takes a bit of courage to do it but it's so rewarding.

We may refrain from praising people for their appearance, achievements or personality because we fear that we might feel inferior in comparison or we just feel awkward or silly doing so. However, when we do allow ourselves to do it, we can create a warm, supportive and friendly environment in which all concerned can learn and grow. Your relationships can become more intimate.

In many workshops that I have facilitated, we have done the Appreciation Circle. This is a Gestalt Therapy exercise where the group sits in a semi-circle facing a single chair. One by one each member of the group sits in the chair and listens while the others in turn say three things that they appreciate about them. These don't have to be particularly personal things but they do need to be specific. For instance, if someone wanted to give a compliment about the person's smile instead of simply saying, "I appreciate your smile", they would say was it what about their smile that they appreciated. Perhaps: "I appreciate your warm, friendly smile."

Everybody finds the thought of sitting in the 'hot seat' terrifying but they have all said afterwards that it was so valuable, not only to receive compliments but to give them too.

I have often thought how wonderful it would be if those people who work in teams such as salesmen or actors would do the Appreciation Circle on a regular basis. Often so much is focused on the 'negatives'; why the sales targets were not met, why someone's performance was not as good as it might have been. I feel sure that it would be more productive if, even just once a month, the team could focus on the 'positives' in their work?

Honest self-appreciation is quite different from the bragging and boasting that we were probably all told when we were children is so wrong. You owe it to yourself to acknowledge your strengths, assets and skills as well as the weaknesses and areas of your personality that you wish to change.

Try making a list of all the things that you love about yourself; your traits, strengths, skills, the ways you do things or don't do things. Head a page with "WHAT I VALUE AND APPRECIATE ABOUT MYSELF IS ..." and see what happens. You may feel very awkward about doing this but try to keep going until you fill the page.

Self-worth is something we are all born with in equal measure. We don't earn it. We cannot do anything to make ourselves more worthy. We just need to become aware of it; accept it. We are all just as worthy as each other.

It took me a long time accept my own self-worth. I felt that I needed other people to witness me doing things and being a certain type of person to make me feel a sense of worth.

I was adopted as a baby by my aunt and uncle. When I was an adolescent, I heard about the tragic circumstances surrounding my adoption. I felt that my birth had caused so much heartache for my natural mother. I took this to heart and ended up feeling that I was some kind of cosmic mistake; that I, quite literally, should not have been born.

It took an incident where I nearly lost my life at the age of eighteen years to wipe out this belief. I was knocked over by a car in a hit and run accident. I suffered serious head injuries and badly broke a leg. It truly was a miracle that I survived. In fact, they called me the 'miracle girl' in hospital. I was unconscious for a few days and semi-conscious for another week during which time I suffered from amnesia. I didn't recognise all the people that visited me but I knew that they loved me because I could see love in their eyes. It was like a light shining within them. I would bathe in the love that I saw in the eyes of, not only my family, but also the doctors and nurses that were looking after me.

After the week of being semi-conscious, I regained my memory of who I was and knew beyond a doubt that life was a precious gift and that I truly deserved to receive it. I have never forgotten that first beautiful experience of seeing the light of love in people's eyes. I still see it and know that love is the essence of us all. The other thing that the miracle of surviving the accident did was that I knew that I was meant to be here - no cosmic mistake. There are no mistakes. I discovered my self-worth. There have been many trials, joys and discoveries since that time but I have always considered that 'accident' to be my opportunity for rebirth.

You don't need such a dramatic awakening to become aware of your self-worth. Value and appreciate yourself everyday. You are a wonderful individual with talents and qualities that are unique to you. Be good to yourself. You are worth it. Be willing to become your very best friend.

2 Making Friends With Yourself

Another aspect of the self-effacing attitude we can have towards ourselves concerns success and achievement.

How many of us are so good about owning our failures but not so ready to own our successes? We play them down, don't want to 'brag'. Why is it that success can sometimes be as embarrassing as failure?

Perhaps this goes back to when everyone seemed to focus on the 'negatives' when we were young. If we got seven out of ten in the class, the attention was on the three we got wrong, not the seven we got right. If we had been good all day but indulged in five minutes of mischief, we may have suffered admonitions about it for hours afterwards.

Sometimes we may strive to be perfect (whatever that means) or are trying to live up to impossible standards that we set ourselves. When we fall short of these, we feel that we have failed ourselves or others. We can be so hard on ourselves; far harder than we would ever be on anyone else. All the compassion, empathy, love and support that we offer to other people can often be withheld from the person that is nearest to us – OURSELVES!

I often say to clients in therapy when they are beating up on themselves in some way, "Just imagine that there is a you sitting in that chair over there and you have just heard that story from them. Now tell me what your reaction would be". They never say, "I would tell them they are stupid" or "I would tell them they are a failure" or any such insensitive condemnation. They very often say that they would like to go over and give them a big hug and tell them that they are OK, that it's alright to make mistakes and to be gentle on themselves.

Tracy was someone that would regularly beat up on herself. She would often say things like, "I must have been very unloveable as a child" or "I know that I must get on people's nerves".

She came into therapy because she was distressed by her compulsive checking behaviour. She had gone through the orthodox channels of psychiatric help only to be told that her childhood was normal and could not possibly be the cause of her problems. Once, when she had been admitted into hospital, she had been given 'sleep therapy' which, I believe, basically means drugging the patient for a given time waking them only to take them to the toilet and feed them. Sounds sinister, doesn't it? All this treatment only served to chip even more off of Tracy's fragile self-esteem.

After a few sessions, it became clear that the root cause of her problems was that she didn't receive the loving approval that a child so badly needs whilst growing up. In fact, quite the reverse was true. She suffered constant criticism. However hard she tried, she never seemed to gain that sought-after approval from her mother. Her compulsive cleaning and checking was an attempt to be 'perfect'. It was almost as if she still had her mother looking over her shoulder looking for the faults in everything she did. There may well have been some misguided logic and loving intent in her mother's behaviour but the effect was extremely damaging on Tracy's self-confidence.

By recognising where her negative beliefs about herself came from and learning to give herself the loving approval that she needed, she courageously began to drop the addictive behaviour that was limiting her life so much. She began to see that she was loveable and really did deserve to be happy and fulfilled.

Sometimes when you notice that you are being hard on yourself, that you are putting yourself down, just imagine that somebody else is in that situation with all the same emotions and thoughts you are having. Imagine how you would react to them. Would you feel compassion? Would you love and support them? Would you be their friend? Allow yourself to be gentle with you.

Become your own very best friend. How you see and feel about yourself will, to a large extent, determine your experiences and the way others see you. You may have had an imaginary friend when you were a child. That friend was just an aspect of yourself that you loved and had fun with. Imagine that now you have a little friend within you. Stop fighting with yourself and treat that inner friend (yourself) as you would treat anyone who needs love and support to help them grow and develop on their life's path. When things go wrong give yourself the benefit of the doubt. Don't automatically blame yourself.

You know that to feel secure in a friendship with someone you need to feel safe and sure that the other person will support you. This provides a secure emotional environment for you knowing that they are there for you no matter what. Build your inner security from knowing that you can depend on yourself to support you no matter what, even when the going gets tough. When things go well be sure to praise yourself.

Don't constantly look for flaws and defects of character so that you can beat yourself up when things don't go quite right. We are not supposed to be perfect. If we were we would not be alive. We would have had our promotion, been awarded our wings and would be in the company of the angels learning to play the harp! It really is alright to make mistakes. So stop criticising and belittling yourself and instead treat yourself with kindness and loving care.

As long as you are battling with yourself you will be creating inner conflict. Treat yourself kindly and politely. Think of the process as being more like this – feeling good about yourself will help you change and grow rather than changing and growing will help you feel good about yourself.

When you can learn to trust in yourself to be supportive, you can relax more in the world around you, take things more in your stride and be able to slow down enough to enjoy the wonders that are always around you. Sometimes with all the hullabaloo of modern living, we can overlook the beauty of a birdsong, the majesty of an oak tree or the peaceful stillness of silence. Cultivate a true friendship with yourself and loving friendships with others will follow as sure as night follows the day.

3 Overcoming the Fear of Loneliness

Emotions are not really negative or positive in themselves. We don't have, on the 'positive' side, such emotions as love, compassion, altruism, generosity, and on the 'negative' side anger, jealousy, hatred, fear and so on. All emotions are positive if they are expressed and released appropriately and are negative if repressed, unexpressed or inappropriately expressed. If we were to substitute the words negative and positive for destructive and constructive, we can probably see that, in some cases, love if not expressed can be destructive and anger if it is released appropriately can be constructive.

For example, if a parent loved their child deeply but never allowed that love to flow into words and actions, the effect would be destructive to both child and parent. The child would suffer from feeling unloved and undeserving and the parent would not be able to experience the joy that a loving relationship with their offspring would bring.

Anger if not expressed does not disappear. It will eat away at the person harbouring it. Resentment will build up and could possibly destroy the chance of having honest relationships or perhaps be manifest in the body as some kind of dis-ease. However, if the same anger were released in an appropriate way, it would lead to a healthy emotional and physical stability and the ability to have more satisfying relationships.

The fear of loneliness is the same. There is a constructive and destructive side to it. If not released it can cause a terrible empty unhappiness and isolation. Unexpressed it can flow into behaviours that are designed to avoid it rather than release it. The constructive side to loneliness can be that it can be the impetus and motivation to look within for your inner resources; to find the stillness in the whirlpool.

Let us look at the causes of this terrible bogeyman called loneliness. It is the child's fear of abandonment and goes further back to the infant's fear of separation from mother. We could even take it back further to separation from the womb or even the soul's disconnection from the spirit world but let us just deal with the child's fear of abandonment for now.

We probably all went through it that first time Mum went out without us: "Are you going to come back?" We may have felt that panic if we were separated from our mother because she or we were put into hospital, or on our first day at nursery school.

It is probable that many times the fear of loneliness has been used as a threat in our home lives and at school. "If you are not a good girl/boy, no one will like you and you'll have no friends." "If you don't learn your lessons, you will never get a job when you are grown up." The ultimate threat is that you will be alone and outcast. We were taught to be afraid of loneliness. Even before we had an inkling of what a state of loneliness or aloneness is, we were told that it was the most frightening thing that could happen to anyone.

Even in our religious teachings the threat is there; that if we do not obey the precepts we will not go to heaven but will be eternally damned – and alone! God will abandon us. He even abandoned Moses for forty years and Christ on the cross felt forsaken. In Revelation you can read about the righteous who are lifted into heaven and the sinners who are left behind. Even in some so-called 'New Age' circles there is much talk about those who are spiritually enlightened being taken up by cosmic beings in space ships and those less fortunate souls left to struggle once more through their evolutionary cycles, perhaps starting once more as rocks and crystals.

All pretty scary stuff. Even if we have never bought into those ideas and paradigms, they may well have had a subtle influence on our psyches adding to the fear of abandonment and loneliness. The threat of it, even as adults, can send us reeling in all kinds of directions rather than face it. We are taught to fear loneliness like the plague.

There are many different kinds of loneliness. The one that springs immediately to mind for most people is simply being alone. For some people that can be a frightening prospect. They cannot conceive of going to the pictures on their own, spending a night in alone or having a solitary lunch in a restaurant.

To overcome this kind of loneliness it is important to get to know yourself, to make friends with yourself in the ways that we have looked at in the previous chapter and to realise that it is not always necessary to have someone else around to validate your experience. A sunset is just as beautiful if you are on your own; a record is just as danceable and a film is just as enthralling. Start to become comfortable with yourself. When you are in your home on your own, try having some fun.

G. K. Chesterton once said, "Angels fly because they take themselves lightly." It is a wonderful quote and I always remind myself of it when I feel I am taking myself much too seriously for my own good. So when you have had enough of wallowing in your loneliness, put on your favourite record and dance around the room, laugh, have a sing-song, pull faces in the mirror, learn to juggle. There's no one looking; allow the child in you to play.

Laughter is a wonderful therapy. Norman Cousins in his book 'Anatomy of an Illness' tells the story of how he cured himself of cancer. He had been diagnosed as having only a few months left to live. He booked himself into a hotel and played loads of comedy videos of Marx Brothers and all kinds of hilarious films. He literally laughed himself back to health.

Research has shown that laughter actually does stimulate the thymus gland, which is an important part of the immune system, so if cancer can be laughed away, I'm sure there are many times when loneliness can be cured with a dose of mirth.

Another kind of loneliness is nostalgia. We have all succumbed to it; luxuriated in it from time to time and it can be very enjoyable. However, if it becomes too much of a habit, it can prevent you from enjoying what is in the present moment or what could be if you allowed it to be. It's good to have beautiful memories but if they cause you dissatisfaction, unrest and an empty longing to return to a past that can never be again, they can cause a desperate loneliness.

This kind of emptiness can often be caused by a sudden change in lifestyle perhaps due to some kind of loss of something or someone. It may be a divorce, redundancy or bereavement. Sometimes the loneliness can cause despair. The despair of feeling hopeless and helpless; a sense of giving up.

Whatever kind of loneliness it may be, they all seem to have one thing in common. The expectations that were held have been disappointed or even exceeded in some way. The loneliness you may feel at a party may be because you expected someone to be there or instead of the security of a job you are given your cards.

If your expectations have been disappointed, just allow yourself to feel the loneliness that may ensue. Give yourself the luxury of wallowing in it for a while. If you give yourself up to it completely and totally to the exclusion of everything else (including making a cup of tea!), as with any emotion, you will find that you will not be able to sustain it for longer than thirty minutes or so. Another emotion will soon supercede it so it is safe to go with it. Remember that it is **only** an emotion and you are so much more than your emotions. Then look at how your expectations were let down and release it.

It seems curious at times that when you finally get the thing that you have been longing for: that salary raise; the proposal of marriage; the new company car or perhaps a significant windfall, there can follow a feeling of emptiness, a kind of "Well, what now?". This is still a sudden shift in expectation even though it is a positive one. In this case, allow yourself to really celebrate it. This will release the empty feelings that may have accompanied your success.

Having many superficial acquaintances can make you feel lonely. Intimacy can only be with a few people at a time but it is this that gives richness to your life, so cultivate a few intimate friendships rather than spreading yourself thinly over many.

Some people may try to swallow the feeling of loneliness down with alcohol or food. Many people who come to me suffering from overeating are doing just this. One way to overcome this is to think of alternative ways of dealing with loneliness; other ways of making yourself feel good. Buy yourself flowers, call a friend, take a walk in Nature, be kind to yourself. Remember that when you are the only person there, you are not alone; YOU are there. Be a person in your own right. Develop your self-esteem, your self-confidence.

Confidence is simply the ability to depend on yourself to cope. The more centred you are, the more aware of your inner strengths and inner peace, the more you will feel that you can depend on yourself and the easier it will be to cope.

There is another type of loneliness which needs to be mentioned. It is what I describe as an exquisite sadness. We may feel this witnessing a beautiful sunset, listening to inspiring music or after making love. It is when you feel suspended in a beautiful melancholy. I first felt this when I was thirteen years old whilst looking out at an incredibly starry night sky. It felt as though I was looking out forever. I felt tiny, insignificant, lonely and yet it was at the same time such a beautiful feeling. I was going through quite a traumatic time emotionally and, in a curious way, it seemed to put everything in proportion.

As I said earlier, loneliness does have a constructive as well as a destructive side to it. So how about the constructive side to it?

We can so often fall into the trap of looking to externals for the source of our happiness. We look for our fulfilment in our relationships or our career and when these are threatened, it feels as though our whole life is in the balance.

The lesson that loneliness can teach us is that when it occurs in our lives, we have the opportunity of looking within. It is then that we can discover all the resources we need. When we can trust that we have access to them at any time we need them, we can begin to depend on ourselves. We can become our own person, aware of the strength as well as the peace and serenity we hold within ourselves.

4 Finding and Editing Negative Beliefs

Now we are going to look at ways you can recognise and clear those negative beliefs that may be holding you back and preventing you from experiencing a true peace of mind.

Our beliefs create our experience. Everything that has been created by human beings has its origins in a single thought supported by the desire to manifest it in some way. For instance, this book you are reading has its origins in the thought that I could do it, and was carried through by my desire to communicate these ideas to you. However, had I let the voices of doubt that I "could not", "should not" or was "not able to" overpower that seed thought, this book would not be in existence.

One of the principles of Huna philosophy (from Hawaii) is that the world is what you think it is. What kind of world do think you live in? Is it an unfriendly place, a loving one or something entirely different? If you have a half bottle of your favourite drink, do you see it as half empty or half full?

We have gathered all the beliefs that we hold about ourselves and life since childhood, some even from infancy. We may have been told by parents or teachers that we were silly or we couldn't sing/draw or whatever. Maybe we were told that if we behaved in that way nobody would love us. We have been told that boys don't cry, girls are too emotional; men are stronger, women are weaker and so on.

We may have received indirect messages that told us that we would always fail or we did not deserve to be happy, loved, successful or wealthy. Maybe we were told that we should not expect to have what we desire in life: "Life's not a bed of roses. It's tough out in the big, wide world." "You can't always have what you want in this life." We have probably all heard similar messages to this. Another, perhaps more subtle, message we may have heard might have been that we should not aspire to reach beyond our parent's level of income, success, happiness, etc. "You should be content with what you have got." "All your fancy ideas. One day you'll come down to earth …" etc., etc.

Maybe we just weren't made aware of our self-worth.

As a result of all this, there is an internal voice that can really disrupt our well-being. It is the terrible 'should' voice. "I should not make mistakes." "I shouldn't complain." "I should be the perfect spouse/lover/friend,etc." "I should be able to cope." The list can be endless. Freud called it the super-ego, others have called it the inner critic, judge or parent. It is the one that gives us a hard time, nags at us, hinders our creativity, spontaneity and very often will drown out the voice of our intuition.

It is an amalgamation of all the authority figures that have had any impact on us in our early lives: parents, teachers, priests, maybe doctors and very possibly a sprinkling of society's 'shoulds'. They become internalised and the beliefs that are created by this mish-mash of ideas become a part of us, colouring our interaction with the world around us. It appears that where our parents finish off giving us our guidelines for life and telling us where we are going wrong, this internal parent takes up the task. The trouble is that it can be more of a strict disciplinarian, critic and sometimes tyrant than ever our parents or other authority figures were. In Chapter One we were looking at how hard we can be on ourselves. This is definitely one of the internal dynamics that is responsible for this.

The first place to start recognising what your negative beliefs are is to look at what your 'shoulds' are. Make a list. If you find it hard, just keep saying "I should …" and see what comes up and write it down. You may be surprised at the restrictions that are operating below the surface.

Bringing negative beliefs out of the unconscious and into the conscious mind will create more choices in your life; will make you feel more in the driving seat of your life. When a belief is unconscious, it will operate subtly in your behaviours, influence how you perceive the world and how you relate to others. For example, for some people when faced with a difficult situation there may be an unconscious voice saying "Well, that's the way life is. It's a struggle." When you bring your belief about the inevitability of struggle into the light of consciousness, you immediately create the choice of whether you simply endure the struggle as inescapable or perhaps search for a way of resolving the situation.

I am embarrassed to say that when I was younger I used to have a negative belief that "all men were bastards and if they seemed not to be, they were just pretending". You can imagine the kind of reality I created with that belief running the relationship show for me. I was like a magnet for all kinds of abuse from men. I was a victim until I took responsibility for my life and realised that the root cause of my attracting disrespect was that I did not respect myself. I worked on changing that negative belief and subsequently developed the self-respect and self-worth I needed. I no longer need to play the victim role and am free to enjoy satisfying and loving relationships.

Whoever it was that said you must be crazy if you hear voices in your head must have been completely crazy if they didn't hear any. We all have a certain amount of internal dialogue.

Kathy started to notice, when she tuned into this internal chatter, that whenever anything went wrong a little voice inside would say: "It must be my fault." It was like a knee-jerk reaction. She worked in a busy advertising agency. One day, whilst her colleague was out of the office, a client of his rang up. He was exceedingly irate about something and the upshot of the phone call was him slamming the phone down on her.

This was the trigger for "It's all my fault. It must have been something I said" but Kathy challenged it this time, worked it through. She deduced that her colleague had forgotten to send some piece of documentation. When he returned, she told him of this and he was able to send the documentation and placate the irate client. The situation was resolved.

The scenario would have been quite different had she assumed the guilt about this situation as you can well imagine. Before she determined to challenge that negative belief, she wore a mantle of guilt that lay very heavily upon her shoulders.

Sometimes, try tuning into that inner dialogue; the 'shoulds', the 'can't do thats', the blame and the guilt and, of course, remember to challenge it.

The unconscious works in symbols and images. It cannot tell the difference between a real and a vividly imagined experience. Therefore, visualisation and image work can be a powerful tool to communicate with it. The visualisation below will help you to discover and edit those negative beliefs that are holding you back from creating a positive future.

It might be helpful for you to tape the visualisations and meditations that are set out in this book or get a friend to read them out to you. The "..." signify pauses, so if you do record them or if someone is reading them to you, it is best to give plenty of time and to speak slowly and softly. Alternatively, I have produced a tape entitled "Creating A Positive Future" that has the following visualisation on Side One.

Editing Beliefs

Make yourself comfortable ... Gently close your eyes and take some nice, deep, easy relaxing breaths ... Think about the rhythm of your breathing ... Imagine that you are breathing in relaxation and you are breathing out any tension from any part of your body, mind ... Allow your thoughts to slow down ... Let your breath take you down to a nice quiet place inside ...

Now imagine that you are walking down a corridor ... Keep walking down that corridor until you come to a door marked 'Unconscious' ...

Pause a while outside this door and realise that inside this room are stored all your beliefs about everything ... They may be stored on manual files, in filing cabinets or on computers ... There will be a helper in the room to give you any assistance you may need to look up and edit any of those beliefs that you may find ...

When you are ready, open the door and walk into the room ... How are your beliefs stored? ... Greet your helper ...

**What are your beliefs on love, money, success, work or rela-
tionships? ... Look them up ... Ask your helper for any help
you may need ... Remember that once you have found those
negative beliefs, you can edit them ... Use the Tippex, cross
it out, use the delete key ... Change them for what would be
more relevant and positive for your life right now ...
And when you are ready leave the room and close the door
behind you ...You can always return at any time whenever
you need to go through the same process again ...
In your own time, take a couple of deep breaths and become
fully present in your body ... Twiddle your toes and fingers
and gently open your eyes.**

It may be a good idea to write down what happened during this
visualisation. It is a bit like reprogramming a computer if you
think about the negative beliefs as being the old program that has
been running so far and the positive beliefs as the new, upgraded
software that is more suited to your growing awareness of
yourself.

Another powerful way of transforming the restricting notions
we have about ourselves is the use of affirmations. They also act
as positive programming. By looking at the negative beliefs you
may have discovered by looking at your 'shoulds', tuning into
your internal dialogue and during the visualisation above, you
can create the affirmations that will cancel them out, as it were.

For instance, if you were to discover a restricting belief that
said you were not loveable, then your affirmation could be "I am
loveable". If you noticed a negative thought occurring in your
mind that labelled the world an unfriendly place, a suitable affirmation would be "I am safe in my world" or "I am finding security within myself". If you are feeling angry with someone, you
could try something like "I am a calm and peaceful person" or
when you are actually with them silently affirm "I greet the light
within you".

Louise Hay in her book "You Can Heal Your Life" explains
much about the use of affirmations and it is well worth buying to
help you with your reprogramming. It is a book that I recommend
to absolutely everyone that comes into my practice.

It is probably not a good idea to work on more than five affirmations at a time and they need to be very clear. If they are too woolly or complicated, the unconscious will have difficulty assimilating them. It is also a good idea if they are in the present tense otherwise the resistant belief to them can postpone the reprogramming to a later date (which may never come). Affirmations need to be positive. For instance, instead of saying "I no longer repress my anger", a more effective affirmation would be "I release my anger appropriately."

When you have the affirmations that seem relevant to you, that resonate as being right, use 'post-it' pads to stick them up around your house, on the dashboard of your car, on your desk at work, wherever you will see them often to remind you of those thoughts that can begin a positive future for you. Also, try saying them to your reflection in the mirror or recording them on a cassette so that you could listen to them in your car or, if you have a personal stereo, whilst shopping.

Here are a few examples that may resonate with you or trigger off something else that is more relevant:

- I deserve to be happy/loved/successful, etc
- Everyday I am becoming more and more of who I can be
- I am finding peace within myself
- I am loveable
- I love and approve of myself
- I am letting go of the past
- It is safe to be me
- I can allow myself to be loved
- I am powerful
- I forgive myself as I forgive others
- My heart is full of confidence and strength
- I hear and see with my heart

Another analogy (I love analogies as you may already have noticed) to illustrate what happens with the process of finding and editing negative beliefs, is springcleaning a cupboard in your home.

You discard everything you don't need, doesn't fit or you just don't like any more. You replace those worn out things with new items that are more suited to your lifestyle, your personality and will help you attain the results that you want. As you clear the clutter from your 'mental cupboard' you will have more room for new discoveries and understandings. You will be able to enjoy a wonderful sense of relief from losing those restrictions that have held you back.

The main thing is to be willing to adopt a more positive way of thinking. Once we have let go of the resistances and are willing to change, life has a way of providing us with the resources to carry it through. You will feel more open to the world and the people around you.

I will close this chapter with one of my favourite stories that illustrate the power of positive thinking.

There was once a prince who had a hunched back. He was very sensitive about his deformity so he rarely appeared in public.

One day, he summoned the court sculptor to commission him to make a life size statue of himself as he would look without his crooked back. He had it placed in a secluded corner of the palace garden and visited it everyday where he would spend some time gazing at it.

As the weeks and months went by his back grew straighter and straighter until one day he summoned to the palace many of the people in the kingdom. They were amazed and delighted to find that the prince's back was no longer crooked. In fact, he looked just like the sculpture in the garden.

He had successfully manifested his true potential by focusing on that positive image of himself.

Remember that what you are thinking now is shaping your future, so be kind and loving to yourself, be gentle, be positive, be strong. You really do deserve to give and receive all the abundant love and joy that life can offer.

5 Clearing the Resistances to Change

By now you are probably more aware of the negative beliefs that have been creating your reality or at least part of it. It may be in just one area of your life, your relationship with money, lovers or bosses. It may be your negative beliefs concerning your expectations of abandonment or rejection have prevented you from getting close or allowing another to get close to you.

If we use the analogy of glasses being our belief system through which we view the world, then what we see will depend on the glasses we are looking through. Changing our beliefs is like trying on a new pair of glasses.

However, sometimes change can be scary even when we know the proposed change is going to be positive. There can often be all sorts of resistances to change just because it is the unknown; uncharted territory as it were. One way to calm any fears or resistances to change is to try out the 'as if' exercise. It is a bit like having a dress-rehearsal before the big show.

If there is a quality you wish to develop such as confidence, strength, self-esteem or peace of mind, or you just want to allow more love, joy or fun into your life, try it out for size. First of all just take a few quiet moments to imagine you are a person with those qualities. Really immerse yourself in the experience. What does your body feel like? How would you interact with other people in shops, at work and socially? Imagine yourself in any kind of situation; see yourself confidently coping and employing those desired qualities.

Then try walking down the road as if you were a person with that particular quality. Again, how does your body feel? Does your back feel straighter? Are you holding your head a little higher? What else do you notice? It is a bit like method acting. When you feel a little braver, try shopping or some other activity as if you were a person with that quality through and through. Notice how you interact in actuality. Afterwards give yourself a pat on the back and congratulate yourself on how you have done. If you are especially pleased with yourself, give yourself a treat to reward your success.

If you ever find this 'as if' exercise difficult; you just can't imagine yourself being able to cope confidently with a certain situation, try using a role model. Think of someone you know (or even a film star, etc.) who has the quality or skill that you wish to develop. Imagine them in the situation, see how they act and what they say, etc. Then imagine yourself using those same behaviours. This will help you to try on those new glasses; try out those new beliefs.

The resistances we can have to change may have been in operation for a long time. We may have set them up as defences at a time when we were too vulnerable, hurt or fearful to allow ourselves to be successful, to love or be loved, to be beautiful, handsome or even just noticed.

We need to find out what those resistances are, then we can set about releasing them. Sounds easy but they may be lurking pretty deep within the unconscious mind. You need to bring them into the light of consciousness to see if they are still relevant. They may well be totally redundant. Sometimes these resistances or defence mechanisms stay in operation for far longer than they need to. Perhaps it is just because nobody has told them they are not needed any more.

If there is something you really want in your life; you want to lose weight or you want to have a relationship, ask yourself why you do not want it. It is not as crazy as it sounds. If you wanted something without reservation you would probably already have it in your life.

For instance, many people come to me saying they want to lose weight. If there were no reasons why they did not want to lose weight, (discounting physiological reasons) it would be easy.

However, the unconscious may be storing all kinds of reasons why the weight is necessary, fear of being attractive and the attention it may cause, fear of being hurt, or it may even be self-punishment.

As far as the wish for a relationship goes, the reasons why not to have one may be a fear of intimacy, rejection, loss of independence or a fear of being dominated.

The fear of success can sometimes be as crippling as fear of failure. It may mean that you are in the front line. You may fear it is undeserved and, "If they find out what I'm really like ..."

So if you have a desire that you want satisfied, an ambition realised or a dream fulfilled, set up a sheet of paper with two columns. In one column write down all your reasons for wanting it and in the other, why you don't. Give yourself plenty of time for this exercise. It may take a while for those resistances to clarify themselves. You need to be very honest and you may find it quite embarrassing. I certainly have at times when I have done this exercise.

When you uncover those resistances you can deal with them appropriately, sort out your affirmations, question the validity of the belief, talk to a close friend or perform some kind of ritual to symbolise letting go of those restrictions. Sometimes just bringing those issues out into the light of day will be enough to release them. It is like when you shine a light on a dark corner it is no longer dark.

The unconscious works in symbols and images so simple rituals are powerful messages to it. One of my favourites is a Native American ritual called 'Throwaways'.

Standing on the shore of a beach, lake or a river bank, you collect some pebbles or stones. Taking one of the stones in your hand, you ask the four elements, the sun and moon, your Higher Power (whatever is meaningful to you) to witness that with this stone you throw away, for example, your fear of rejection. One by one, release all your resistances while casting them into the water. It feels really good.

The first time I did this, I was with a friend on Penzance beach at about eleven o'clock at night. We were triggering each other off about different resistances. She would say hers and it would remind me of one that I needed to release and I would do the same for her. We were picking huge pebbles for the really sticky resistances and crying out "Ho" as they plopped into the sea. I don't know if anyone witnessed those two mad women on the beach that night. It felt a very powerful experience but was also lots of fun.

Another ritual that may be effective in releasing resistances might be writing them down on a piece of paper and burning them out in the garden or in the sink. As the smoke rises and dissipates into the air, really imagine that your resistances are dispersing with it.

Yet another could be lighting a candle and dedicating it to the release of those things that are holding you back. Of course, you could also light a candle and dedicate it to what you wish to create in your life.

Our resistances are all that is standing between where we are now and where we can be when we allow ourselves to be open to the possibilities that are waiting for us. Having cleared the blocks, you can then begin to manifest the reality you want. You can simply allow it to happen.

6 Creating a Positive Future

There are all kinds of techniques for assisting this process. A favourite one for many people is the Pink Bubble technique. You visualise what you want to manifest, surround it in a beautiful pink bubble of light and allow it to lift up into the air giving it up to the universe.

Another simpler but equally dynamic one is to visualise your goal in tableau form frequently during your day. Just flash it up into your mind's eye. Alternatively, see the reality you want to create as you would see a scene in a movie. See all the details as clearly as possible, make the scene as rich and colourful as you can. Think of it in the present tense, as if it were happening exactly as you want it to be right now. Allow yourself to feel all the joy, all the happiness and satisfaction that you will feel when it manifests in your reality. Remember your thoughts are creating your reality so allow them to be positive and your emotions and, of course, your reality will follow suit.

I will tell you an amusing thing that happened to me when I was trying to create a certain reality. I imagined, in tableau form, a yellow Volkswagen beetle parked outside my house. I had the image of my little yellow car very clearly in my mind's eye. One Sunday morning, I looked out of the window and there it was exactly as I had visualised it parked right outside my house. The drawback was it was my neighbour's new car. He was proudly taking photographs and obviously loving his new acquisition. There was a part of me that felt like going out and telling him as

I had manifested it, it was by rights mine. Needless to say I refrained. I had omitted in my visualisations to have the keys and log book in my hand so all is fair in the manifestation game. I see him on a Sunday morning polishing it and giving it lots of loving tender care so I couldn't possibly resent his good fortune. So take my advice and be specific in your visualisations!

When we are feeling good about ourselves we can have such a positive effect on our environment and the people in it. We really can create a positive world around us. Of course, the same would apply if we are feeling negative. We will spread our gloom around with us. It is not a cliché. We really do have impact on our environment. We may want to deny this fact, wish to think that we are pretty insignificant, but we do have impact.

Let me give you a very simple illustration of how we affect others in our world.

Imagine a scenario where a family is having breakfast together; starting their day. Mum has not had a good night's sleep. She is not feeling too good about herself, the toast gets burnt and she trips over the cat. She shouts in frustration at her husband and cuffs her son around the ear for laughing.

Her husband goes to work in a terrible mood and takes it out on a colleague who in turn passes it on to her poor secretary. The colleague goes home at the end of the day feeling unappreciated and ends up having a row with her boyfriend. Maybe a similar situation happens to the secretary. The son goes to school feeling picked on and plays up in class. It's the last straw for his teacher as he is coming down with a cold and ... well, you get the general idea.

All those people indirectly affected by one person, let alone all the people she would have been directly affecting during the course of her day. Imagine the scenario differently. She is feeling positive, looking forward to the day and all the fresh challenges that it will bring to her. She feels centred, calm and loving. How different her environment will be and the effect that she will have on the people in it. She will be wearing very different glasses to view the world than the ones that she would have been wearing in the first scenario.

I heard a little while ago that scientists have realised that there is no point that can be measured at which the light of a candle ends. The light particles get smaller and smaller the further away from the source of the light but it appears it radiates out into infinity. Hearing this, it made me think of our inner light. That also shines out endlessly. We can nurture that light and allow it to glow brightly in our environment and know it is shining out even further than we can possibly imagine.

When I am feeling good about myself, feeling centred and happy, I find I am more giving and open to the people I meet. When I am shopping, I will thank the assistant for their help and enjoy their smile in return for my appreciation. I find I have enjoyable and loving encounters the whole day through.

I remember one day, however, when I had to buy some envelopes from a local stationer's as I didn't have time to go into town. I was complaining to myself that I didn't want to go there because I thought they were unhelpful and unfriendly. I noticed what I was doing - programming myself for an unpleasant experience. I gave myself the same advice I would give someone else in this situation and reprogrammed the scene. I imagined going into the shop and receiving friendly and willing service. All the way there I maintained a positive attitude to the shop and guess what happened? Yes, they were helpful and friendly.

I think that in some curious way people telepathically read your attitude towards them. It is an unconscious thing. It is known that it is only about fifteen per cent of communication is verbal. The rest is body language, facial expressions and who knows what we are communicating with the energy our moods and thoughts create.

I am sure we have all had the experience of noticing the dampening effect a person in a 'black mood' can have on a group of people. Alternatively, we know the effect a bright shiny and enthusiastic person has when they enter a room. They radiate their light and lift everyone's spirits. Interestingly enough, the root of the word 'enthusiastic' is from the Greek word enthusiasmos which translates as 'inspired by the god'. It figures when we think about the impact that a person with such a quality can have on everyone around them. The positive energy they exude is contagious.

Think about the quality you need to develop in order to bring more love/joy/success/abundance, etc in to your life. Then write at the top of a blank page "If I had ... (the quality) I would ..." and see what comes up. This will help you to project this positive quality into your future. When you have completed this, write down a few ways in which you might bring more of this quality in to your life, what actions you could take, and affirm that you are willing to take those actions.

We really do have the choice. The choice to be happy, successful, fulfilled and allow love to flow into and out from our lives. We can make the choice to value and appreciate ourselves, to be our best friend, to love and approve of ourselves and to allow these positive feelings to spill out into our environment. We can make the choice to be at peace with ourselves and moment by moment create a positive future.

7 From Warrior to Adventurer

One of the most insidious negative beliefs we may hold is that life is a struggle. It can seem as if we have no choice but to bear with the hardships life may throw at us. However, we really do have the choice. We can look at our need to struggle and start to develop our ability to act and not just react, to learn to trust ourselves, to make the transition from warrior to adventurer and to enjoy the simple pleasures of life we may overlook when we are hell-bent on struggling.

It says in the Bible that "the love of money is the root of all evil" (1 Tim. 6:10). I don't know about evil but our beliefs and attitudes to it can certainly cause us a lot of confusion and unease.

I remember about twenty years ago attending a talk by that wonderful gentlemen, Sir George Trevelyan. I cannot remember much about it although I'm sure it was a fascinating talk. There was one thing, however, that he said which stuck in my mind for years before I received any inkling of what it might mean. "Money is the physical manifestation of the energy of love." It just rumbled around in my mind all those years. It was as if I had put it on the back burner until I was ready to understand it.

I had always had an uncomfortable relationship with money. I felt it was not a nice thing for an artistic, sensitive or spiritual person to be concerned with. I thought it was much too materialistic. I had this notion that it was only alright to have enough to get by and no more; if I had more, someone else might have less. Added to this, I seemed to have a fixed pattern of always struggling to make ends meet. I was a single parent so I accepted this as the way life was and probably always would be. Those were the glasses I viewed this particular aspect of my world with. "Life is a struggle but I will muddle through somehow and make ends meet." And I did, by the skin of my teeth at times.

No, this is not going to be a section on "Think yourself rich". I think there's quite enough of that sort of thing about, but the taboo subject of money needs to be looked at; our negative beliefs and expectations about abundance.

My expectations were that it would always be a struggle to pay the bills, feed and clothe my daughter and myself, find money for my education, etc. Therefore, my reality supported this totally and I battled my way through life.

Then five years ago, after struggling to find the money to go on an Applied Kinesiology seminar, I was staying overnight in a hotel in Bath. It was then that it dawned on me. It was like a light bulb going on in my head. I realised I had the choice; if I was brave enough I could really give up the struggle.

As I lay on the bed in my hotel room that night, I reflected on the whole issue of ownership and came to the conclusion it really is a myth. There is no such thing. I thought about the travels of a pound coin. It never stays in one place too long. It moves around from person to person, flowing into shops and purses, into banks and out again. It was then I remembered that little phrase of Sir George's. Money seemed to flow in the same way as love. If it flows freely it can be a positive energy and if it is blocked or dammed up it can become negative.

I let this idea rumble around in my mind for a while and then I brought into my awareness all I 'possess' and I substituted the word ownership for guardianship. I became a guardian of the money I have in the bank, the pictures I have on my wall that give me so much pleasure, my computer and every last piece of furniture. I felt that giving up my concept of ownership and replacing it with responsible guardianship, freed me to begin to trust in life's processes more: to trust that what I need or truly desire will flow into my life if I allow it. **Allow** being a key word.

I looked around the hotel room and saw quite clearly that while I was staying there, I was a guardian of everything in the room. I did a meditation that night that may be useful to you in making the shift from ownership to guardianship.

Becoming a Channel

Make yourself comfortable ... Taking nice, deep, easy relaxing breaths ... Allow your mind to become still ... If a thought comes into your mind just notice it and let it go ... Imagine your thoughts to be like leaves floating on a surface of a stream ... watch them floating by ...

Now bring into your awareness all that is in your possession ... money in the bank ... your home ... your furniture ... bric-a-brac ... all your precious things like your favourite pictures ... souvenirs, gifts ... all you can think of ...

Now offer them up to whatever you conceive your **Higher Power** to be ... give it all up without exception ... Release every last thing ... even the clothes you are wearing ...

Now accept those things back from the universe ... You are taking them back now as a guardian ... Affirm you will be a responsible guardian for the abundance of the universe ... and whatever else flows into your life ... You will continue to be a worthy guardian ...

And when you are ready bring yourself back to the room and gently open your eyes.

I did this meditation every Sunday morning for a few months, offering up all that I have along with all I had earned or acquired that week. It felt as though I was opening up a channel for abundance. No, I didn't suddenly become rich but I gradually stopped struggling. I began to trust that abundance like love can flow into my life as easily it flows out if I allow it to.

It may seem an airy-fairy idea but it works. Whenever I feel that doing something like going on a residential workshop in Devon would be so right for me, I trust I will receive the means to do it.

It doesn't mean I just sit back and wait for it to fall into my lap. I do what I can to earn it but sometimes it does seem like magic when, at the eleventh hour, a debt I may have forgotten about is repaid or I suddenly have an incredibly busy week in my practice. I no longer fret about bills and I no longer struggle to pay them.

Sometimes I love to muse on a world economy that has substituted guardianship for ownership. Just imagine, nation states being worthy guardians of the earth's resources which are located in their country. A deep psychological, emotional and spiritual shift would have occurred. Peace would really be possible when you consider the fact that most of the world's conflicts have been and are about greed and the tactical 'ownership' of resources.

Another source of struggle is the negative belief (there's no getting away from them) that it is the only way to learn life's lessons. I think we have probably all said at some time after we have suffered a difficult period in our lives, "Well, it was tough but I sure learned a lot from it all."

It is fine that we can use life's adversities to our advantage as long as we recognise that it is not the only way to learn and grow. We really do have the choice to grow through joy and happiness as well.

If we have the unconscious belief that we need a crisis in our life to stretch us and help us learn life's lessons, we may find when things are going well for us we will unconsciously sabotage our happiness. So that is a belief that is well worth rooting out and editing.

I used to regard myself a spiritual warrior battling through life courageously casting out the demons and dragons of doubt and adversity (I exaggerate!). Joan of Arc was my guiding light as I struggled through the battle zone of life. Phew, what hard work it all was!

Eventually I stopped waging war against what I saw as negativity and started to see myself as a spiritual adventurer. It is quite a shift; from battling to adventuring. It requires surrendering the need to be in control and allowing yourself to flow with life more. It doesn't mean becoming a will-o'-the-wisp being blown by the winds of life. It means learning to trust in yourself.

If you trust yourself, the issue of trusting others hardly comes into the equation. When you trust in your ability to cope with any situation in which you find yourself, you just need to learn discernment in your dealing other people. If you learn to trust in your discernment, you can relax into the flow of life and allow the great adventure to unfold around you.

Sometimes it requires a certain amount of courage to make the choice to let go of the ways you have employed to keep control over your life.

One of those ways may be 'people pleasing'. This could be doing or saying things which you feel will have the desired effect of others approving or liking you. You may strive to fulfil the role you think is required of you (whether it is or not is a different matter). The 'good person' role can become a trap for the person filling it. It requires a rigid self-control which becomes stifling. For example, you may not be able to express your feelings if you feel your lover, partner or boss would not approve or understand. Also, you may find it difficult to say no to something you do not really want to do for fear of being rejected in some way.

There is also the caretaker role which requires not only self-control but also a certain amount of control over others. What can start off as a well-meaning intention to help, can sometimes turn into being obsessively hooked into another person's problems to the point of being totally out of touch with one's own feelings. It can also mean that, in the attempt to help the other person, one can end up controlling them and putting your own happiness on hold: "When he/she is better, sorted out, healed, has a job, etc, **then** I/we will be OK."

Another more subtle but nevertheless powerful way of controlling others is playing the martyr. It is one of the most manipulative behaviours there is. When a martyr says, "Don't worry about me, I'm fine." with that pained look on their face, it is hard for anyone not to get drawn in to the game of worrying about them and doing whatever they can to alleviate their suffering. It is a sure way to get attention **and** control.

The sad thing is that these mechanisms of control, even if someone is acting the overt tyrant, are all coming from a lack of trust in life's processes and poor self-esteem.

If it is not ourselves or other people that we try to control, it may be our world. Sometimes we feel if we don't hang on to things with a tight hold, everything will fall apart. However, it is one of life's paradoxes that when you let go of your need to control as well as all the subtle manipulations that go with it, you are not an acquiescent passenger but you can feel more in the 'driving seat' of your life.

I truly believe whenever I am experiencing any kind of inner conflict it is because I am trying to exercise some kind of control over my life, maybe a relationship or another person. I have either lost my trust in myself or respect for another person and as a result, I am trying to manipulate events or the other person involved. I may feel it is for all the right reasons at the time but when I own and release my need to control, I am able to see the whole situation with a new perspective.

An adventurer takes things in their stride, doesn't have preconceptions about how other people are going to react or how things are going to turn out. They allow themselves to be fully in the present moment. They have the humility to realise that things and people may be completely different from what they were yesterday.

When you can see your life as an incredible adventure that is revealing itself moment by moment, what a warrior or struggler may see as a misfortune or setback, you will see as an opportunity that you are willing to accept. You will be able to use it to learn and grow through discovering the message that the situation is offering you.

I often award myself a whole day specifically devoted to having an adventure. It may be to go to London for the day, take a picnic in the country or go on a long bike ride with a friend. When you are on an adventure, it doesn't matter if you get on the wrong train, it rains or even if you get a puncture because it can all be a part of the adventure. When you watch children playing you can easily see their sense of adventure. We just lose it somewhere along the way to adulthood but it is so rewarding to recapture it.

Ending the struggle is a bit like an SAS officer who has been dropped on to a roof by helicopter, abseiled down the wall and crashed through the window only to find out that the door was open all the time. He realises there was an easier way but the struggle was all he knew or expected even though it was his own home he was entering.

We can give up struggling and allow ourselves to be excited by the newness of each day. Live the adventure to the full. Make the choice to be happy, to have fun, to allow life to nurture you and feel the gratitude for all it offers you. The choice is really yours to make.

8 *Healing the Inner Child*

Contacting and healing the child within is a powerful way of helping to break negative patterns of behaviour and healing the emotions.

A couple of years ago, a friend of mine who was working in a school came across this poem on the staff notice board. I think it is anonymous. It says so much about how a child is affected by the emotional climate in which they are brought up. It is called "Children Learn What They Live".

"If a child lives with criticism,
    He learns to condemn.
If a child lives with hostility,
    He learns to fight.
If a child lives with ridicule,
    He learns to be shy.
If a child lives with shame,
    He learns to feel guilty.
If a child lives with tolerance,
    He learns to be patient.
If a child lives with encouragement,
    He learns confidence.
If a child lives with praise,
    He learns to appreciate.
If a child lives with fairness,
    He learns justice.

If a child lives with security,
  He learns to have faith.
If a child lives with approval,
  He learns to like himself.
If a child lives with acceptance and friendship,
  He learns to find love in the world."

Carl Jung once said that "in every adult there lurks a child". It is the part of the personality that strives to develop and become whole. Contacting the inner child can enable us to find that lost world of imagination, fun and spontaneous joy.

The two aspects of the inner child that we shall be dealing with in this chapter are the vulnerable child and the magic child.

The vulnerable child is the part of us that may have suppressed its natural creativity and aliveness in order to win the love and approval it desperately needs as it is growing up. Healing this aspect of ourselves is such a rewarding process to go through as it leads to being able to find that spontaneity, joy and aliveness we all too often lose during our growing years. Why do we lose these precious aspects of ourselves?

Well, at around the age of five and coinciding with the start of our school education, we had to learn to adapt to our surroundings and the people in it. At school we were immersed in 'better thans' and 'worse thans'. "She isn't as good at drawing as me." " I wish I could run as fast as he can." We were constantly being compared to our school chums and at home we were possibly compared to our brothers and sisters. We had to compete for attention.

Also, if we don't receive the love and approval we need, the conclusion we can come to is that we are not loveable and are not worthy of approval. We just don't have the sophistication of thought to reason that Mum's not feeling too well or Dad is worried about the financial affairs of the family or even that the two of them are not getting on too well at the moment. This is when the negative beliefs that we form about ourselves as a result can carve themselves deep into our unconscious.

The most important thing about considering all of this is to understand we now need to parent ourselves; to love and approve of ourselves. The aspect of ourselves that needs the most of our love is the vulnerable inner child that was suppressed so many years ago.

The vulnerable inner child often manifests in our lives when we are ill, tired or have been rejected or fear rejection. I am sure we can all think of times when we have felt that vulnerability.

This is a simple visualisation for you to contact that aspect of yourselves, communicate with it and find out its needs.

Meeting Your Inner Child

Allow yourself to relax ... Allow yourself to gently drift into gentle relaxation ... breathing easily and deeply, concentrating on the rhythm of your breathing, allow your breath to relax you even more ... Do what you do to help yourself relax ...

Now imagine yourself in a beautiful park on a bright, sunny day ... All your favourite flowers and trees are in this park ... butterflies fluttering over the flowers ... bird songs in the trees ...

Somewhere in the park is your inner child waiting to meet you ... It may be up a tree ... on a swing ... sitting on the grass ... or on a park bench ... Look for it ...

When you find it notice how old it is, what it is wearing, the expression on its face ... Ask it its name ... it may have a favourite nick-name that it likes to be called ... Greet it in what ever way seems appropriate ...

Now get to know him or her ... Ask your inner child how it feels ... How it feels about its place in your life right now ... about its hopes and dreams ... its doubts and fears ...

Now ask it if there is anything that you can do for it, either in your everyday life or here in the park ... Remember, don't make empty promises ... It has probably been hurt by those in the past ...

Now give it a big hug ... tell it you love it ... that you will always be there for it ... to give the love and approval it needs ...

Say goodbye ... just for now ... promising that you will give your inner child a special place in your life from now ... And when you are ready gently open your eyes.

A similar visualisation is on a tape that I have produced entitled "Contacting the Magic Child Within".

If possible, find a photograph of yourself as a child, the closest to the age, and maybe dressed the same, as they appeared in your visualisation. Put it up by your bedroom mirror and give it lots of love every morning and evening.

Try to make a habit of inwardly asking your child what its needs are. Try devoting a day or if you can't spare a whole day, an afternoon or even an hour to your child. Inwardly ask what it would like to do. Have fun. Have an adventure. Be free and happy. Be creative. Tell yourself, your child, that you **are** loveable and you **are** worthy of approval. Find the joy in being a loving parent to your inner child.

I have been doing inner child work with people for many years now and know how dynamic it is but a couple of years ago what seemed like a miracle happened to a client that gave me such incredible joy. Pippa came to me because she thought there may be a combination of psychological as well as physical reasons for her inability to conceive.

At the consultation, using kinesiology to diagnose, we ascertained that her pituitary was out of balance and a nutritional regime and supplementation was sorted out, and because of some emotional issues in her childhood that she spoke of, counselling also seemed appropriate.

She came to see me weekly and on the fourth session we did the above visualisation and I advised, as above, devoting a day to her child the following weekend. She has a wonderfully supportive husband who encouraged her and together they went to London Zoo to be kids for the day. They both had lots of fun. Well, to cut a long story short, **that** turned out to be the very day that she conceived. Healing her inner child seemed to be the key that unlocked the problem. While Pippa was pregnant, she and her husband came on an Inner Child workshop and their story was inspirational to everybody there.

Pippa and her husband and their beautiful baby girl have become very dear friends of mine so now I can enjoy watching the beautiful little 'miracle' child growing and receiving all the love and approval that she could possibly ever need.

Another way of contacting your inner child and finding out its needs is a written exercise. With your dominant hand, as the nurturing parent, ask your child how it feels, what it would like you to do for it and then lovingly pass it to your inner child to answer through your non-dominant hand. This way you can develop a loving dialogue with your inner child.

Lucia Capacchione has written a marvellous book called "The Power of Your Other Hand". In it she gives lots of exercises, using your non-dominant hand, where you can contact aspects of your inner child and much more. It is well worth getting.

When you have healed your vulnerable inner child, you can contact the magic child within you. This is the dreamer in us. It knows the world of fairies and spirits. It is the part of us that can dare to dream and believe; can fearlessly seek and enjoy adventures. It is the spiritual adventurer within us. When we get in touch with this magical child, we are able to reach beyond the restrictions we may have had to accept while we were growing up.

The magic child is never really lost, it is just separated from us by our adult mind. All the dreams we once had, that maybe we couldn't share or, if we tried to were ridiculed, are still there deep within us. Our adult mind is often concerned with fears brought through from yesterday making us fear tomorrow. Sometimes it can miss what is happening today. Contacting the magic child enables us to find our creativity in the present moment.

The magical child can help us to allow ourselves to play, to experience a sense of wonder and awe at the world around us. Notice a young child watching a ladybird on a leaf or a train passing or see them picking up a handful of sand and letting it trickle through their tiny fingers. They are totally absorbed in the moment. It is as if nothing else exists for them at that moment and I guess it doesn't. The child consciousness within you can help you to see and feel what your adult mind may miss. Remember lying on the ground watching the clouds changing their shapes from dragons to tigers, from castles to trains? Treat yourself sometime to a spot of cloud watching. Give yourself completely to the experience.

Take a moment to think about those wonderful moments when you were very young when you were totally absorbed by something or someone. Maybe you saw fairies or angels (many children do). Think of times when you felt totally free and connected to everything around you. It may have been when you were in the countryside, playing with an animal, singing, making things, painting or just being in your favourite place. I remember when I was very young, I used to dance. It didn't matter if I had music or not because I had music in my head. Sometimes I would dance myself into fantasies of being a ballerina or a princess.

Therefore sometimes when I want to recapture the essence of my magic child, I dance. I put the answer-phone on, move the coffee table out of the way and dance barefoot around my living room. If I am feeling strung out about something, it is a sure-fire way of lifting my spirits. I can dance my way into joy.

Remember a way that can reconnect you with your magic child. Take a bit of time out every now and then to experience this magical aspect of yourself. It can bring a wealth of creativity and fulfilment to all that you do.

9 *Letting go of the Past*

Sometimes we can be carrying a lot of excess baggage from the past. It may be packed with painful experiences, a sense of loss or through a nostalgia for 'better days'. These ties can drain energy and vitality away from us.

Letting the past loose is setting yourself free. It's just a pity it is so much harder than it sounds. All the mystics, philosophers and psychologists have always told us that to get to where we want to go, we need to let go. So why is it so difficult? Why do we hold on?

Firstly, we need to look at what we have invested in the past. Sometimes the pay-off to hanging on to a painful past is that we can throw it up as an excuse as to why we cannot move on. We may use the past to manipulate others. We may also feel that we need to rationalise the past. "If only I had a good education, **then** I would be successful." "If only my parents had not treated me so badly, **then** I would have a fulfilling relationship." "If only you hadn't said those terrible things to me ...", etc., etc.

Letting go of these things would take away our excuses. Perhaps the thought is that, "I would have been perfect if only those things hadn't happened to me". Maybe the idea of being 'perfect' is scary. Hanging on may help us to avoid moving into the unknown. "Better the devil you know."

There comes a point with many people in therapy, after they have been releasing the pain of the past, when they get scared of how they can cope without their negativity. They feel that even though they don't want to hang on to their victimhood or whatever their old pattern is, how else do they deal with their life? The old ways may not have brought them happiness but at least they coped somehow with it.

It is a natural fear but the way through it is to integrate the past. We cannot let go of something until we own it. We need to recognise that the past is an integral part of our path. Whatever it is, it has led us to here. It is not the whole of us but it is part of who we are. In the same way that you are a unique person with individual qualities and talents, you have a unique history. Acknowledge your history. Glean the gifts it has given you. If you have had suffering in your past, it has probably given you compassion for others. If you have had joy, it has probably given you the ability to help others to find the joy within their own lives.

On joining the college where I studied psychotherapy, I was impressed by the diversity of people on the course. They were from all kinds of social, political and economic backgrounds and a wide range of ages too. However, the one thing that seemed to be common to us all was that we all seemed to have had our fair share of trauma in our lives; some had suffered bereavement, divorce or separation, others had lived through traumatic childhoods or had suffered miscarriages. We had all learned from our histories and sincerely wanted to pass this on to others by working in a caring profession.

It may be difficult to let go of the anger that the past has created. Again, we cannot release this until we own it; allow ourselves to feel it, express it appropriately and let it go. The 'throwaways' I mentioned in Chapter Five could be useful in releasing the past and all the emotions that tie us to it.

Letting go of our need to blame can sometimes be tricky. It is a defence system. I'm sure we have all experienced a time when, to deal with the pain, hurt or anger caused to us by someone or something, we resort to blaming the other person or even society as a whole. It may seem to make it easier on us but it cuts us off from our true feelings.

Make a list of the gifts that the aspect of the past you want to release has given you; the understanding and wisdom, the compassion and empathy you can share with others. Thank the past for these treasures.

Also, make a list of why you are holding on; what you will lose by letting go. This will be quite challenging but very informative to you about the pay-offs to hanging on that are serving you. Then make a list of all that you will gain from freeing yourself from it. Finally say Goodbye to the dream that you had or may have shared with someone.

You can apply this to events or your emotions about people in your past that are preventing you from enjoying your life in the present moment to the full.

Letting go of a past relationship is a difficult emotional issue for all of us. We can often feel we have failed in some way whether we or the other person finished the relationship.

Again, look at the nature of the gifts that the relationship has given you. Acknowledge the essential qualities you have gained from the relationship as a part of you; a part of who you are **now**.

In the same way as our history is unique, so too are each one of our relationships. We come together with another on our life path as each of us is developing and evolving. We learn from each other those lessons we need to learn from the interaction that occurs in the relationship. Sometimes we are attracted to someone because they possess the qualities that we really need to develop in ourselves which is why we often witness the phenomenon: 'opposites attract'.

Each relationship will change in mood and direction from time to time. They need to be fluid, to flow with the shifts and changes that occur with the passing of time. Trying to keep things as they were when you first met and felt 'in love' will cause stagnation and conflict and can kill the growing dynamic of the relationship. Accusations of "You've changed. You are not the man/woman I met" can start to get hurled about. We all change as we grow and we need to acknowledge this as well as respecting the changes in our partner too.

It is said the only thing that is constant in this world is change and this is especially true of relationships. At times these shifts will bring you closer together. At other times they may cause you to drift apart. There is no failure. Perhaps at the end of a relationship, you have both learned all you can from each other and perhaps you can move it on to a new level that is more relevant to you both. At times it is the most loving thing to do – to release each other and continue on your individual life paths.

It is so hard to do; to release someone with love. As I said earlier it may seem as if it is easier to do it with blame, anger or resentment. Something I have found helpful in the past when I have been going through this kind of situation is whenever I think of that person, especially if it is with negative emotions, I affirm sincerely, "I release you, (their name), with love" or "I now release you, (their name), to your highest good". It has helped me to resist the temptation to bring in my armoury of defences.

Below is a meditation to help you release a relationship with love and forgiveness. You can use it whether it is a parent, an ex-lover or husband, friend or anyone with whom you feel a strong emotional tie you wish to be free from.

Releasing Past Relationships

Make yourself comfortable ... Breathe easily and deeply and begin to let go of any tension in your body ... With each exhalation allow your body to relax even more ... Now take a nice deep breath and as you breathe out, allow yourself to slip down to a nice quiet place deep inside you ...

Now imagine there is a cord attached from just below your navel that is connecting you to that person that you wish to release ... Picture them clearly in front of you ... Know that the cord represents the emotional charge between you ... Now have a dialogue with that person ... Ask them what is the nature of the contract between you ... What was it that your coming together was to teach you ... Perhaps you also wish to know what they needed to learn from you ... Take as long as you wish ...

Now say to them "I forgive you (if this is appropriate) and I release you from my life with love. I release you to your highest good and I ask you to release me to mine." ... Allow yourself to feel the emotional charge between you being released ...

Now pull out the cord ... and let the image of the person fade from your mind's eye ... Bathe the area where the cord was attached with golden light ... and rest for a while before

you return your awareness back to the room where you are relaxing ... and gently open your eyes ...

This is a powerful meditation. You may only need to do it once or a few times to start feeling free from the emotional bonds that have tied you to that person.

Cathartic letters can be useful too. They are not to be sent. Write "Dear..." and allow any stuff to come up uncensored even if the language is foul! Let those emotions out. Keep writing until you feel it has all been said and then read it out loud just once. Then put the letter in a draw for a week. If you need to go back with a "P.S. And another thing..." then do so. After a week take it out of the drawer and read it through. You will be surprised how much the bite has seemed to have gone out of the emotions. Then have a ceremonial burning; outside or in the sink (wherever it is safe). As the smoke curls up and dissipates into the air affirm that you are releasing those emotions from your life.

If you write a letter to a loved one who has died, tell them how much you love them. So many times when someone we love has died, we can feel so guilty about the fact that we never told them how much. Tell them all the things you maybe never said but wanted to. Do the same for anyone who has died with whom you feel that there is any kind of unfinished business. Conduct a special ceremony for them that is intimately yours. For instance, lay out some flowers, light a candle and some incense and say a personal prayer celebrating their life and thanking them for all that they gave you. You don't really lose them because the gifts that you gleaned from your relationship with them will always be with you. In this way you can free them and yourself to continue on your paths without each other.

This actually helped me so much to let go of the grief that I felt for a very dear friend of mine that died many years ago. I somehow felt it was wrong to let go of the grief, that it was kind of disloyal to stop suffering over the loss of our friendship. Every time it came round to his birthday or the date he died, I seemed to go through the mourning all over again. When I eventually focused on the precious gifts our friendship gave to my life and realised that these gifts would be with me for always, I knew that it was okay to let go of the hurt that I was holding on to. I conducted a special ceremony, blessed him and wished him well on his new path. I now have beautiful memories but they don't hold me back from forming new intimate friendships any more.

In the next chapter, we will be looking more deeply at what is probably the most vital ingredient of letting go of the past – forgiveness, forgiveness of ourselves, others and the past.

10 Forgiveness

Before we look at what forgiveness is and the ways in which we can do it, let us consider what it **is not**. It is not condoning another's actions. It doesn't make it right. It is also not forgetting or giving absolution.

Forgiveness is letting ourselves out of the prison that the emotions tying us to that other person have created for us. It is setting ourselves free from the burden of resentment. It will break the final hold that the emotional bonds of the past can have over us. It will restore our emotional balance.

Forgiveness can be the key to attaining an inner peace and being more fully in the present moment. When there is someone who we need to forgive, we are judging that person as they **were**, not as they may be **now**. To break free from the past, we need to be willing to forgive. The willingness to forgive allows us to break free from the shackles of the past and can transform our thoughts from fear into love.

Let us take a look at the resistances we may have to being willing to forgive.

Many of them will be similar to the resistances that I spoke of in the previous chapter. We may be holding on to our need to blame, excuses for not moving on or being perfect or not being willing to let go of anger. Another very common cause of the unwillingness to forgive is the feeling that reconciliation will be obligatory, "If I forgive them, will I have to be friends with them, invite them round for dinner?"

As I said earlier, forgiveness is setting yourself free. If you were to forgive someone, you are not suddenly obliged to like them. They still may not be the kind of person you would wish to socialise with. You have the choice whether you reconcile with them or not. It may happen quite naturally but it doesn't matter if it doesn't. The important thing is to release the emotional charge between you.

Own and release the resistances to forgiveness and then you can get on with the business of actually doing it. If you have more than one issue of forgiveness, the resistances may be different for each of them. However, when you can feel that you are truly **willing** to forgive, then you are ready to begin the process.

It is important to remember first and foremost to forgive yourself with **any** issue of forgiveness. I work with many adult survivors of child abuse and one thing that seems to be common to all is that they blame themselves in some way. They may feel that they deserved it or they are angry with themselves for allowing it to happen.

When you were a child or adolescent or maybe even more recently, you didn't have the resources that you now have at hand to deal with hurtful or traumatic situations. So forgive yourself for allowing that thing to happen. There may have been nothing you could have done to prevent it. Also forgive yourself for what you may have done or not done. You know better now but you didn't then (even if it was last month!). Deal with the self-blame: "If only I had done this or I had said that" etc. Punishing yourself or another for something that has happened in the past will never contribute to a healing process. Be compassionate with yourself.

If it is something that occurred in your childhood that you need to forgive, find out, using the visualisation in Chapter Eight, how your inner child feels about it; how they feel about forgiving that person or event that happened. This will help you to resolve and heal the child's emotions. The same visualisation can be done for your inner adolescent.

As far as forgiving the other is concerned, start with the 'why' they did it and let the 'what they did' follow in its own way. The reason many people cannot find it in their hearts to forgive, is that they feel they could never forgive **what** the other person actually did. It may be so terrible or they just feel it is not really up to them for some reason to forgive the action. Don't get stuck on this. Think about why they did it. Consider the person's background, perhaps their childhood, the lack of love in their life. It will help you see that person in their own right and, as I said, the 'what' will follow on later. If it doesn't, it doesn't matter. Forgiving the 'why' can still set you free.

Another written exercise for you. Writing things down is so much more helpful in clarifying the emotions that surround issues than just letting it ruminate around in your head. Write down first what you forgive yourself for in a particular situation and then what you forgive that other person for. Be as specific as you can.

The meditation given in the previous chapter is an excellent one for forgiveness. Another may be to visualise the person surrounded with golden light and affirm to them something like, "I forgive you as I forgive myself" or "I forgive you and release you from my life". Continue to visualise that person being bathed in golden light until it completely surrounds them like a golden bubble. Then allow it to lift up off of the ground and float up and away until it is out of sight. Watch the golden sphere disappearing and feel the release of all the last vestiges of constricting emotions with it.

To help you to focus on the energy of forgiveness, it may be helpful to have an object such as a crystal that symbolises your willingness to forgive. Pour your desire to forgive into that crystal, meditate on it and carry it with you to remind you of that desire.

People that make us angry; those we find it hardest to forgive, are probably our greatest teachers. They can show us where our prejudices are as well as the areas of ourselves we need to shine the light of consciousness on. They will challenge our comfortable ways of being and thinking and make us question our right to judge and point the finger at anyone.

There must have been so many times in all of our lives that we have looked back at what may, at the time, have seemed a horrendous circumstance, but we recognise in retrospect, was an important turning point in the course of our lives. It may have been a powerful impetus for positive change. When you take that retrospective view of your life's events, the whole issue of right and wrong sometimes becomes very blurred especially when you consider the lessons and opportunities that may have been gained. Here is a story that illustrates the futility of judging from a narrow perspective.

There once was a poor farmer who lived on his own with his son. His only possession was a horse. His neighbours tried to convince him to sell the horse saying, "It's bad to have a fine horse when you are so poor. Sell it." The farmer simply said, "I don't know if it is a good or a bad thing. All I know is I have a horse."

One day his horse ran off and his neighbours said, "There, we told you it was bad to have a horse. Now he's run away and you have nothing." The farmer simply said, "I don't know if it's good or bad. All I know is that my horse is gone."

Then one fine day, his horse returned with five mares following him into the farm. The neighbours, when they heard the good news said, "It is a good thing your horse ran away because now it's come back with five more." The farmer said "I don't know if it's a good or a bad thing. I just know now I have six horses."

While his son was breaking one of the mares in, it kicked him and broke his leg and the neighbours said, "It's is a bad thing your horse came back with those mares. Your son has now been injured and cannot work on the farm." The farmer said, (you've guessed it) "I don't know if it is a good or a bad thing. I just know my son has broken a leg."

The king was gathering an army to fight a battle in a foreign land and all the young men apart from the farmer's son were enlisted into his army. They subsequently all lost their lives in the conflict. The neighbours said to the farmer, "It was a good thing your son broke his leg because he is now alive and all of our sons are dead." The farmer simply said, "I don't know if it is good or bad. I just know that my son is alive."

It is a wonderful story, isn't it? It reminds me that sometimes I just need to forgive the past; to forgive life for not always being easy or as I would want it to be and that perhaps it is really all part of my learning process in this lifetime.

Forgiveness takes practice but once you make the choice to set yourself free from the prison the emotions of resentment have held you in, you can allow more love to flow into your life. It may not be particularly from the person whom you have forgiven (although that may well be the case) but it will flow from others around you. There will seem to be more room in your heart somehow. When your resistance to forgiveness dies something very beautiful is born within you. It is your increased ability to love and, equally important, your capacity to allow yourself to **be** loved.

Having cleared a good deal of the debris from your life, it will be so much easier to find that constant and nurturing stillness within yourself. In Part Two, it is this we shall be looking at; ways of finding the stillness in the whirlpool of life.

Part Two: Finding the Stillness in the Whirlpool

11 Relaxing Mind and Body

In this chapter, I will be discussing how and why stress may occur in our lives and will be giving you some simple relaxation techniques you can use in your everyday life to help you to unwind, let go of the distractions of the day and relax your mind and body.

It is so important every now and then to set aside the worries or excitement of our lives and simply let go and relax. Many people have the erroneous belief that taking time out to relax is doing nothing; the old work ethic comes to the fore and tells us that we should be **doing** something. But relaxation **is** doing something. It helps us to recharge our batteries and in so doing, we are better equipped to get on with our busy lives more effectively.

Not all stress is negative. For example, the kind that is caused when you fall in love or with the excitement we feel anticipating a pleasure or reward. However, the stress that debilitates or produces depression or anxiety needs to be changed and while you may not be able to change your environment or situation you **can** learn to change your reaction to it.

The causes of stress are many, from noise to resentment, from fatigue to emotional upsets. You may well have inherited your reactions to stress in the sense that you could have learned by watching how your parents dealt with stressful situations. For instance, you may have seen how tense your father was when he was driving or how your mother got bad-tempered when she was worried about something.

Modern living itself can be stressful. It comes at us from all directions. We walk down the High Street and we are bombarded with slogans such as "Buy one and get one free", "Buy now and pay in January" or "Bargains! Don't miss out". We go into a bank or post office and we may feel calm and relaxed but the person behind us may not be and we will certainly feel their anxiety and impatience as they wait in the queue. It is hard to stay unaffected by other people's stress.

Another source of stress that comes from living in the era of communications can be the global awareness that we have now. On the one hand, it is wonderful to be linked, in a matter of minutes to people on the other side of the world via the telephone or satellite but on the other, we are constantly aware of all the tragedies and maladies of the whole world. I sometimes feel our emotional development lags behind our technological advancement. In one century, we have gone from living in close-knit communities to the awareness of a global village and the ensuing responsibility we may feel for the whole human family.

It is a double edged sword. The communication advancement has enabled us all to learn about many different cultures and to contribute in helping developing nations but it can also give us a a sense of helplessness when we witness the human tragedies in the form of famines, droughts and wars that are shown on our television screens every night. We may feel our little efforts can't do much in the face of such huge problems.

When I feel that kind of futility, I remember the analogy of the candle flame I gave you in Chapter Six. I think of my light shining out into the world along with my hopes and prayers for peace.

I also remind myself that change will happen in the world by the power of each person making positive changes within themselves. So please don't ever think of the journey to self-awareness as being a self-indulgent path to tread. As you change and evolve as a fully fledged human being, becoming all you can be, you will contribute to changing the world.

The greatest changes that have happened in the advancement of humanity have been initiated by individual people acting as beacons on the path of progress. Think of the effect on the world that people such as Gandhi had with his message of change through peaceful means or Emmeline Pankhurst, the pioneer of woman's suffrage. They were people just like us who had the courage of their beliefs and stood firmly in their truth. Our impact on changing the world may not be as dramatic as the kind made by those two but it will be no less significant.

Sometimes we can be holding tension in our bodies without even realising it. We can be lost in thought and our shoulders can be so tense that they can end up around our ears or we can be gripping the steering wheel so tightly our knuckles go white. It is such a waste of valuable energy. Holding tension in the body can really be hard manual labour.

A lady came to me a while ago whose right shoulder muscles had gone into spasm. She was an elderly lady who had been nursing an invalid husband for many years until he died a few months before she first came for treatment. She had coped wonderfully all the time she was caring for her husband. Although his death hardly came as a shock to her, as soon as he died it was as if all the tension she had been coping with had finally caught up with her. She came in the door looking as if she was doing an impression of Quasimodo with one shoulder about six inches higher than the other. However, when I helped her to enter a deep relaxation, I watched her shoulder drop and relax in front of my eyes. It was an incredible sight.

She had been taking muscle relaxants, having physiotherapy but all she really needed was to learn how to relax. She had a few sessions with me during which I taught her a few techniques (which I shall be giving you later) on how to release the tension in her body and her shoulder remained where it should have been. This along with some counselling enabled her to gradually adapt to her new life style.

Every now and then check your body over for tension; top to toe as you may check over an engine looking for faults. If you find any, put your awareness into that place and let it go. Take a deep breath and release the tension as you breathe out. If you find it difficult, tense the area as tightly as you can and then release it.

Relaxation is a physical skill which can help you to overcome physical, emotional and mental tension. As with any skill you want to acquire, it needs practice. Eventually, it will become more and more an integral part of your whole life.

Slower, deeper breathing will move you to a calmer, more

centred space. You will feel more in control of your emotions as a result.

Abdominal Breathing

Breathe right down into your stomach. Don't just use the top of your lungs as we do so much of the time. Deep abdominal breaths. Practise it. Put your hands on your abdomen and feel it rising as you breathe in and falling as you breathe out. Now place your hands on your rib cage. If you are doing this correctly, there should not be as much movement. Find the natural rhythm of your breathing and try to get the in-breath the same length as the out-breath. Feel yourself relaxing.

This kind of breathing will be useful in any potentially stressful situation. Also, the more control over stress you can achieve the more confidence you will feel in yourself and the stronger you will become as a person.

Here is another useful relaxation technique you can use when you have a spare five minutes to unwind.

Five Breaths

Make yourself nice and comfortable ... Close your eyes ... And take five deep breaths ... On the first deep breath, allow all of the muscles in your head, face and neck to relax as you breathe out ...

On the second deep breath, allow all the muscles in your shoulders, arms and hands to relax as you breathe out ...

On the third deep breath, allow all the muscles in your legs and feet to relax as you breathe out ...

On the fourth deep breath allow every muscle from the top of your head to the tips of your toes to completely relax ...

On the fifth deep breath use this as the signal for you to go into a deeply relaxed state for five minutes ...

What I do on that fifth breath is put myself somewhere really nice; on a beautiful, golden sandy beach, on top of a mountain or in a clearing in a pine forest. I also find it helpful to play some relaxing music.

I have always been amazed how my unconscious seems to know how long five minutes is. There have been times when it has seemed much longer but when I have opened my eyes, it has always been around the five minutes. I guess it must be that you programme the mind as you go into relaxation on that fifth breath.

Other people find it easier to relax by concentrating on various parts of their bodies from their feet upwards; tensing and releasing the muscles until their whole body is completely relaxed. Do whatever works for you best.

The adrenal glands sit on top of the kidneys and are under the direct control of the nervous system. They are our buffer against stress. They prepare the body for action. I am sure you have heard of the 'fight or flight' syndrome. Well, it is the adrenals that are responsible for this. It is not important to know all of the intricate workings of the adrenals, only to understand that an anxiety state or panic attack is a combination of physical as well as psychological symptoms. In considering this, we can easily see the interdependence of the mind and body.

If we constantly fail to deal with tension appropriately, we teach the nervous system to overreact which causes the adrenals to pump adrenalin into the system. We will feel 'wired up' and what we end up with is a psychological state with physical symptoms. In effect, when we learn to relax, we re-educate the whole nervous system.

I read a research report a little while ago which said that when you are going through stress you can use up to seven times more vitamin B6 in the body than normal. I think it is safe to say, in the light of this, that if you are experiencing any kind of stress in your life, it would be advisable to be taking a B6 supplement to stop the drain on the reserves of this essential vitamin in your body.

Poor diet can also contribute to a diminished capacity to deal with stress. There are many excellent books on nutrition that can help with this or it may be advisable to consult a nutritionist that can advise on your diet if you suspect this is an area you need to attend to.

Whatever you do don't 'should' on yourself about stress. "I should not get so stressed out." "I should be over my divorce by now", etc. Most of us have to deal with stress in some form or another. We just have to learn ways of dealing with it effectively. There are the few people that are naturally 'laid back' and nothing seems to ruffle their feathers but they are the exception rather that the rule, and anyway, who knows what goes on beneath their calm exterior?

12 Using the Breath

Many people ask me how can they stop distracting thoughts coming into their mind while they are relaxing or meditating. The answer is you cannot stop them coming in but you can quite easily release your attachment to them once they come into your awareness.

If you are a visual person, you could imagine a little box and place those thoughts one by one in the box and close the lid knowing you can look at them later if you wish to. Alternatively, you can imagine your thoughts to be like clouds floating in the sky and watch them dispersing or leaves floating on the surface of a stream drifting by.

Of course you could easily bring yourself back to relaxation by simply becoming aware once more of the rhythm of your breathing. Being aware of your breath will bring you back to the present moment. Those irritating thoughts which intrude on your still moments are invariably to do with the past (even if it is only a few hours ago) or expectations about tomorrow.

There are many breathing techniques that can help you to relax or can be used as a prelude to meditation. In this chapter, I will give you a few that you can try out and see which ones suit you best.

This is one that I adapted from a Yoga exercise.

Circular Breath

Make yourself comfortable ... taking deep, easy and relaxing breaths ... imagine as you are breathing in, you are breathing in up the right hand side of your body ... and as you breathe out, you are breathing out down the left hand side of your body ... In right up to your head and down and around your feet ... Imagine you are making a nice circle of relaxing breath right around your body ...

Now imagine you can turn that breath to light ... The light may become your favourite colour ... feel that soothing, healing light travelling right around your body ... (don't worry if you are not visual, just imagine what it would FEEL like to have light travelling around your body) ...

Now extend that light outwards ... With each out-breath extend that light out farther from your body ... making a wide aura of light around your body ... In this way you have created your own special protective aura you can use in your everyday life when ever you feel affected by stress ... or you just want to relax ... Just get that breath travelling around your body, turn it into light and extend it outwards and you will be able to remain calm and relaxed within ...

Enjoy the relaxation for as long as you wish and gently bring your awareness back to the room and gently open your eyes.

This is Rhianon, my daughter's favourite. A little while ago, she was working for a software development company and it was quite a stressful job. Every now and then, she would leave her office and go into the Ladies toilets. Rhianon would sit in one of the cubicles and do the Circular Breath for a few minutes after which she was able to go back into the fray refreshed and ready to cope with the situation at hand.

Sometimes when things get frantic, if you take a few minutes out for calming yourself, it can save you hours. If you feel calm and relaxed, you are more efficient and effective in all you do as well as being a happier and, most probably, healthier person.

This next exercise is a Yogic one to stimulate the brain and the nervous system and is excellent when your head feels muzzy or you feel your nerves are a bit jangled.

Alternate Nostril Breathing Exercise

Sit with your back nice and straight with your neck and head in a straight line with your spine, shoulders slightly back but relaxed ...

Breathe steadily and easily. Try to get the incoming and outgoing breaths the same length. Observe the natural rhythm of your breathing ...

Now press the left nostril closed with your thumb and inhale through your right nostril ...

Remove your thumb and close your right nostril with your forefinger and exhale through your left nostril ...

Without changing fingers, inhale through left nostril ...

Change fingers, exhale though the right ...

Inhale through the right and exhale through the left, and so on ...

This may seem all very confusing but once you get the hang of it, it is very easy and what is more important – it works! Mind you, you may get some funny looks doing this at your desk at work, behind the wheel of your car or in a queue at the super-market checkout. It is an amusing thought that perhaps there are many more people than just Rhianon using work's or public toilets for recharging their mental and emotional batteries with such techniques.

Something I use as a way of calming my thoughts in order that I may relax or meditate, is using the breath along with a visualisation.

Ebb and Flow

Close your eyes and allow yourself to relax ... pay attention to your shoulders... This is an area where we carry so much tension... Allow them to drop and relax ...

Think about the rhythm of your breathing ... become aware of the air passing though your nostrils and throat as you are breathing in and out ...

Now imagine that you are standing on a beautiful sandy beach ... watching the waves rolling in on the shore ... Continue to observe the rhythm of your breathing ... and begin to notice that the ebb and flow of your breath as you are breathing in and out is matching the ebb and flow of the waves as they roll in on to the shore and pull out to sea... Each breath ... each wave ... ebbing and flowing is helping you to relax more and more ...

Each time you feel a distracting thought pulling you away from relaxation ... simply bring your attention back to the ebb and flow of your breath synchronising with the ebb and flow of the sea ... Imagine waves of relaxation flowing right through your body and let go ...

When I am working with a few crucial affirmations, I do this exercise to relax my mind and body and then silently, I make my affirmations to the rolling sea. I also find it a great exercise for helping me drift off into sleep.

I will give you one more breathing exercise and then I think you will have enough to choose from for now. In later chapters, we will be looking at various meditation techniques that will also be using the breath.

Rhythmic Breathing

Sit with your spine, head and neck in a straight line and your hands resting on your lap ...

Inhale slowly for the count of six and hold for the count of three ...

Exhale slowly for the count of six and pause for the count of three before you inhale again ...

Repeat this a few times, taking care not to tire yourself out at first ...

You can increase the count for the in and out breaths,

remembering to half the counts on the retention and pause between breaths. However, it is more important to pay attention to the rhythm of your breathing than it is to try to increase the number of counts that you use for this exercise.

13 Meditation

Over the years I have come across many ideas that say you should not meditate if you are angry, distracted or in any state of mind that is not calm and collected. However, if most us were to wait around until we were in the 'right space', we may not get a lot of meditating done (at least I don't think I would). In any case, if we **were** calm and collected perhaps we would not feel we needed to meditate anyway, and if we are upset, surely **that** is the time we need it most.

Of course, it may be harder to find the motivation when life is hectic and you are feeling frazzled, but when you allow yourself the space to meditate, it will certainly help you to see your way through it all. Meditation is a tool that you can use to still the mind, to turn off the internal chatter and just allow yourself to be. We are such **doers** in our lives. It is such a luxury to allow ourselves a bit of time to just **be.**

You may also use it to contemplate a certain aspect of life or to access your inner wisdom. It can be silent or you may chant. There are many meditation groups that meet on a regular basis but it can be practised alone. You can follow one particular discipline or try many until you find the one that suits you best. So the only rule to meditation is that really there are no rules. It is as individual as we are.

As I said in the last chapter, you can use various breathing techniques as a prelude to meditation. They can help you move into a quiet space where you can rest a while and enter a meditation.

Here is a meditation using the light of a candle as a point of focus;

Candle Meditation

Relax your body and still your thoughts ... follow the ebb and flow of your breath ... and let go ... Focus your attention on the candle flame for a while and then closing your eyes, bring the image of the candle's light into your mind's eye ... Hold it there for a while imagining that the candle flame is flickering within you ... It is your Eternal Light ... Direct the light to your eyes to help you to see with love ... to your ears to help you to hear with love ... to your mouth to help you to speak with love ... Now direct the light throughout your body, perhaps to specific areas for healing ... and then send it out to members of your family, friends ... and anyone or any situation that you feel needs healing ... Then bring your attention back to the flame within you and finally open your eyes to focus on the lit candle in the room.

The thoughts that may encroach on your meditations on a regular basis can show you the areas of your life you need to deal with, will show you what still needs to be cleared out of that mental cupboard. So don't beat up on yourself for not being able to keep your mind clear for long. The mind can sometimes feel like a racehorse that is difficult to keep still. Simply make a note afterwards of what came up and perhaps you could do a bit of the kind of reprogramming that we looked at in Part One.

Here is one of my favourite meditations;

The Pink of Love and the Blue of Peace

As always, make yourself as comfortable as possible wherever you are ... Close your eyes and breathe deeply and easily ... Breathe right down into your belly ... feel your stomach rising as you breathe in and falling as you breathe out

... and just think about the rhythm of your breathing as you allow yourself to relax and drift into gentle relaxation ...

Now imagine as you breathe in, you are breathing in the colour pink ... a beautiful rose pink ... the colour of unconditional love ... If you find this difficult, imagine there is a pink cloud in front of you and you are breathing the pink vapour into yourself ... Otherwise, just imagine what it would feel like to breathe that lovely pink into your body ...

Feel the pink of love filling every part of you ... relaxing every cell and tissue of your body ... allow it to fill you and let go ... You are breathing in all the love that surrounds you ... the love that holds the universe together ...

Continue to breathe the pink of love into yourself but now as you breathe out, imagine you are breathing out the colour blue ... The most beautiful sky blue you have ever seen ... The colour of peace ...

So you are breathing in the pink of love and breathing out the blue of peace ... Think of your body as a transformer ... transforming the pink of love into the blue of peace ... and feel an inner harmony and healing taking place within you ... Allow yourself to drift deeper and deeper ...

Rest a while within this inner harmony until you wish to bring your awareness back to the room ... back to your body ... and gently open your eyes ...

You can use this meditation to simply 'enter the Silence', as the Seneca Indians called it, or as a prelude to reflective meditation.

So what is reflective meditation? With this kind of meditation, you can use the rational mind to good use. Keep it occupied as it were. This way you can avoid it meandering off into trains of thought which might lead you away from your meditation. It can help you discover more about yourself and the ideas and concepts you may want to have clarified. This kind of meditative concentration is what the Buddhists called the practise of **Samatha**.

For instance, if you wish to know more about the quality of courage, trust, honesty or love, allow yourself to relax down into a quiet place deep within yourself in which ever way you have found that works for you. Simply allow any thoughts and feelings concerning that quality to come up to the surface. Look at them from all views round and give yourself plenty of time to fully contemplate this quality. When you feel satisfied that you have fully explored it, open your eyes and perhaps you would want to write down any insights that you received. Read it through and think about those insights. Also notice what other thoughts may come up as a result.

Most mornings, I pick an angel card out of the Angel Pack from the Findhorn Foundation. There are 52 cards in the pack and on each card is written a different quality such as Tenderness, Joy, Abundance, Trust or Love, etc with an accompanying illustration of the angel of that energy. I pick a card and use the particular quality to reflect upon during my meditation. The instruction leaflet with the deck encourages you to welcome the angel, breathe it into yourself and listen for any message which may come through. The ones I pick out always seem to have some kind of relevance to my life at that time.

There are many other cards you could use in the same way such as Lynne Andrews' Power Deck, The Medicine Cards or Inner Child Cards. These cards are not so much oracles as they are wonderful tools to provide you with a positive focus for your reflective meditation.

Reflective meditation can also be useful when you have a difficult decision to make or when you feel you are at some kind of turning point in your life. When you are in meditation, silently present the question you need to ask or focus on your problem or dilemma and wait to see what comes up.

This can be so helpful in clarifying issues; to being able to 'see the wood for the trees'. I'm sure that we have all experienced a situation where we have been trying hard to find a solution to a knotty problem but to no avail. We give up, go to sleep and wake up the next morning with the answer uppermost in our mind. Reflective meditation utilises this curious unconscious mechanism in the most constructive way.

It may be a good idea to establish a particular place in your home where you can do your meditations. Some place where you can perhaps light some incense and a candle and maybe some fresh flowers or whatever you feel would make it special. If possible, set aside a particular time for meditating. This will establish a habit in your mind. It doesn't have to be for long at first. Even if it is only for ten minutes a day, it will be so beneficial.

The traditional Eastern schools of meditation urged their followers to sit in the lotus position to meditate (a position that I personally find impossible to get myself into). They may also have advocated all sorts of ascetic practises to cleanse the mind and promote the detachment of desires. Whilst I do not decry any of these paths to enlightenment, they may not be the right path for all of us to follow especially when we need to blend them into the routines of our everyday life.

You can meditate in any position that is comfortable for you whether it is sitting in a chair, crossed legged on the floor (in lotus position if you are more supple than myself) or lying flat. Just try to keep your spine as straight as you can.

Make the commitment to yourself that you will find the time to attune to the space within you where you can find refreshment and awareness.

Be eclectic and try many different ways of meditation until you find the right one for you. There are many books and courses on various methods of meditation. Don't get stuck on a particular method. If a particular method which has worked for you for a while starts to seem limited or incongruent, don't worry or blame yourself for not doing it right. It may be the changes you have made in your inner life will mean that another method would be more relevant to you.

The process of growth is a dynamic one so trust your heart and be flexible. All the answers you require in your life are within you. Simply go within and ask for your direction.

Meditation is a powerful practice because it teaches us a discipline of our minds and can give a focus to bring us into the here and now. Without the regular nurturing that a meditative practice can provide, we can feel like flotsam on the turbulent sea of our lives.

I will finish this chapter with a beautiful meditation on finding the stillness within.

The Standing Stone

Allow yourself to drift into gentle relaxation in which ever way works for you ...

Now become aware of the weight of your body ... Notice how each limb is flopping onto the place where you are relaxing ... Using your imagination encourage yourself to feel really heavy ... It's as if the forces of gravity are getting stronger and stronger ... Now it is as if you are no longer made of flesh and blood but are turning into stone ...

Feeling as if you were stone, imagine you are an ancient standing stone set upon a hill ... Your feet are set deep into the earth and from your position you can see the landscape for miles and miles around you ...

As this ancient standing stone you have an unchanging stillness which fills your being as the world changes all around you ... There is the daily change of day into night ... There are also the changes of the seasons as Spring goes into Summer ... Summer into Autumn ... Autumn into Winter ... and Winter returns to Spring ... And as year succeeds year so the centuries flow by ... and as time goes past even millennia ...

And then there are the changes created by man as he lives on the land changing things according to his needs and desires ...

You are still and silent as you observe all that is happening ... you don't judge the changes in any way ...

This silence is not a superficial quality it reaches deep down within you ... Follow this silence inwards ... into that vast inner universe within you ... Ahead you see a light to which you feel drawn ... Follow this light ... enter it and allow it to envelop you ... wrap you round like a cocoon ... and rest within this light ... within your stillness ... This is a place where you can find peace and quietness ...

So rest awhile in that place of stillness ... Allow yourself to absorb the nourishment you need from that light for as long as you wish ... and then gently bring your awareness back to the place where you are relaxing ... bringing the knowledge of the stillness with you back into your waking state ...

I often feel that quieting my mind and stepping into the stillness within is like coming home to a real fire. The razzmatazz of the world is going on outside while I warm myself by the hearth of my inner light.

14 *Being Fully in The Present Moment*

When we bring ourselves fully into the present moment, whatever we do can be a meditation.

Now is really all there is; the only reality. We can get so caught up in all the stuff we bring through from yesterday as well as all the fears, anxieties and expectations about tomorrow. Of course, it is important to deal with and release our past so we can allow our tomorrow to be all that it can be but the healing which occurs happens in the present moment, using the inner resources available to us at that time. In other words, what we are really healing is how the past is affecting us **now**.

One of the greatest rewards we gain from releasing the past and our fears of the future, is that it can help us be so much more aware of what is happening today.

Awareness is a happening in the here and now. Now is all we can truly be aware of. Even our reflections of the past are happening in the present moment.

There are four kinds of awareness. One is an awareness of our physical environment; what we see, taste, hear, touch or smell. Another is our sensory awareness, what we feel inside our skin; muscular tension, itching, comfort, discomfort, well-being, etc. The third is that vast realm of mental activity such as imagining, thinking, interpreting, guessing, comparing, fantasising, remembering, anticipating, explaining, rationalising and so much more. The fourth kind of awareness comes mysteriously into our consciousness in the form of hunches, inspiration, gut feelings and a deep knowing. We may call it our intuition or inner wisdom.

It is the awareness that is behind all the machinations of our minds, behind who we think we are and behind the mechanism of time. It is the stillness that is always constant and true because it is life itself. Although our life changes moment by moment, that pure awareness just is. It is the eternal now and we can tap into it at any time we choose to. The other three kinds of awareness can lead us to this realm in many different ways if we follow them with full consciousness.

Living a true present has its rewards. We can enjoy the actual working out of our needs as well as the satisfaction from gratifying them. For instance, the satisfaction of eating does not have to be just for the experience of satiating our hunger. We can enjoy the taste, texture and smell of our food as well as the whole process of biting, chewing and swallowing, the colours on the plate as well. Try this out as an experiment. Eat a whole meal with total awareness of each mouthful. Take your time and savour the whole experience. Eating is so often an unconscious activity, simply a necessary function. Use your awareness like a spotlight to follow the whole process and see what you can discover.

You can even apply this to the menial tasks in your life. Try doing something like the washing up as if you have never done it before in your life. Remember what fun it was to do the washing up when you were a young child? Rediscover the experience and forget about the drudgery of doing it.

Sometimes, I find it fun when I am in town, to imagine that I am an alien who has just landed on Planet Earth. I am seeing the High Street with all its shops, delivery vans and all the busy shoppers for the very first time. I am always surprised how much more I notice about the town that I live in when I play this game. I notice architectural details above the shop fronts I had never seen before. I am more aware of sounds and colours and smells.

There is a Buddhist practise called Walking Meditation. It is simply what the words suggest. Take yourself for a walk in nature and use it as a meditation. If you live in a city or town, I'm sure there is a park not too far away from you. During the whole walk, stay with your experience; the sounds, smells and sights that you see from moment to moment without judgement, criticism or comparison. If you see a beautiful flower or hear a birdsong, simply surrender to the experience. If you find your thoughts straying off and away from what is happening in the present, gently bring your awareness back to what you can hear, see or smell. Say to yourself "What is happening right now?" and tune in.

I love watching birds in flight. I feel as if I can totally lose myself when I see them twisting and gliding on the air currents. It feels as though there is a piece of me up there with them. (Have you ever read "Jonathan Livingston Seagull" by Richard Bach? It gives some wonderful descriptions of a gull's flight.) It is also such a wonderful meditation to fully experience the beauty of a flower in bloom. It is so delicate, so intricate, so perfect. It is one of nature's finest mandalas.

So much of the time we can be so rooted in our identity of who we think we are; our 'somebodyness' as Ram Dass calls it, that we can get out of touch with what is happening right under our noses. When we allow the awareness of the velvety softness of a rose petal, the sound of a child's laughter, the serene and graceful beauty of a swan or the way our muscles relax when we luxuriate in a hot bath, our somebodyness dissolves and all that is left is awareness. We let in the magic that is inherent in each moment.

This next exercise is based on one from Emmanuel's Book and is a beautiful meditation on staying in the Now using the breath.

Staying in the Now

Close your eyes and relax your mind and body ... Focus your awareness on the present moment ... Become aware of the rhythm of your breathing ... its ebb and flow ...

Consciously follow your breath as you breathe in and out ... Now with each inhalation, breathe into the next moment of your life ... and as you breathe out, breathe out all that ever was ... all of your past ...

Let each inhalation bring you to the present moment ... and let each exhalation free you from the past ... Continue this for a little while ...

Then in between each inhalation and exhalation pause a while ... Don't strain or force it ... allow and observe the natural pause ...

In this pause you are touching the Eternal Now. No Past. No Future. Just Being.

It is good sometimes to stop and simply notice what is happening in your experience right now. What may you be missing?

If I were to become aware of the present moment as I am writing these words, I am aware of the hum of my computer, a plane is flying overhead, I sense a little tension in my shoulders as I tap the keyboard and as I shift position, I feel the tension release. I am aware of thinking about what you will think about these words and a slight anxiety that you may not resonate with what I am saying. I release this thought and notice my cat sunning himself in the window and enjoy the look of luxuriant pleasure he appears to have. In entering into his experience, I momentarily dissolve and return to consciousness when I record the experience. This exercise from start to finish took just a few minutes.

A useful exercise that you can do when you feel you are getting caught up in worries or negative thoughts, is to write down all you are immediately aware of; on all the levels of awareness. Write down what you can feel and sense inside and outside of your body, any worries, fears, hopes or anticipations. Notice the thoughts and feelings that take you out of the present moment and those that lead you back into it. By writing down all you are experiencing you will probably make some interesting discoveries.

You will notice how transitory your experience is. You pass from one emotion to the next like a butterfly fluttering from one flower to another. Just observe and record it without judging or censoring. Use the spotlight of your awareness to follow what is happening in your experience. This way you may discover the root of what may be worrying you and from this you can allow any solutions to surface. Just brainstorm ideas and resolutions on the predicament you are involved in.

Practising techniques which can guide you into the here and now can help you to develop greater self-awareness as well as an increased awareness of the world around you.

15 Grounding and Centering

I have just sat down to my computer to start this chapter after being outside doing a bit of gardening. Sometimes it takes a lot of motivation for me to go out and actually get stuck into the job of weeding and mowing the lawn, etc. I can find all sorts of reasons why I have not got the time or the energy to do it but when I do make the effort, I feel so rejuvenated afterwards. It is not just the smug feeling of having done it (although I do allow myself the luxury of wallowing a while in that as well).

For me it is such a good grounding exercise especially when I feel a bit scattered. In the summer, I like to do my gardening barefoot so I can really feel the earth under my feet.

The earth is a living, breathing organism that we depend upon for our existence. Modern living can cause us to become so out of touch with her nurturing energy. If we live in towns or cities, we can go for days, weeks or even months without our feet even contacting the earth. We walk on the layers of concrete, paving slabs or tarmac that cover the earth like a shell.

In the past few years, we in the West have become aware of the ways the native American Indians perceive their existence. From this we have received a fresh outlook and a timely reminder of the interdependence of all living things.

The native American Indians have always sensed their connection with the earth. When their lifestyle allowed them to express this connection fully, they intuitively knew when it was going to rain or when the rains would end. If they were out on the plains, they would know where to find water and where they could find buffalo. Their survival depended on their atunement to and connection with the rhythms of the earth.

An essential part of their culture was the honouring of and gratitude to Mother Earth. Nothing that was taken from the earth was taken for granted and nothing was wasted. If an animal was killed, every single part of it was used and prayers were offered up for the spirit of the departed animal. They felt themselves to be an integral part of the planet and through this connection, they had access to the healing energy from the earth itself, not only in the form of herbs but from the raw energy itself.

We have become so distanced from that essential connection. We buy the fruits of the earth pre-packaged, pre-picked and pre-slaughtered. This distancing can also damage our sense of gratitude for the gifts the earth offers us daily. I am not suggesting it would be better for us to 'return to nature', as it were. I am far too attached to my refrigerator and washing machine for that! I just remind myself from time to time that the earth blesses me with so much and I allow myself to feel the warm glow of gratitude to her in return.

The earth's energy is a wonderful resource which is available to us all. We can draw on it simply by opening ourselves up to feel it. A powerful way we can open up to that energy is by grounding ourselves. This simply means becoming consciously aware of our connection with the earth in some way.

A simple grounding exercise would be to stand (preferably barefoot) on the naked earth. Feel your feet on the ground. If you are standing on grass, feel the coolness under your feet. Be aware of how you are standing. Is the weight more on one foot or is it evenly distributed? Stand strong. Draw the earth's energy in through your feet up into your body. It may be easier to imagine doing this with your in-breath. Perhaps you could even imagine that there is a nostril on the bottom of each foot and breathe the nurturing energy from the earth up through your feet and feel it filling your whole body.

One day my daughter came home from work looking decidedly ungrounded. Her energies seemed scattered all over the place. She was chattering away, not really focusing on what she was saying at all and consequently was not making an awful lot of sense.

I sent her out on to the lawn to do this exercise for a little while. She came back into the house a few minutes later so much calmer and was able to tell me what it was she was trying so hard to reveal to me earlier.

Tree hugging became very popular a few years ago. It is another way of grounding. It certainly feels great to do but you can get some very funny looks from passers by! So hug a tree if either you are on your own or you really do not mind the attention you may attract. However there are many other ways of grounding using the help of trees.

When I was a child, I discovered that trees can be wonderful friends. I remember having two tree friends in a nearby wood. One was an oak tree and the other was a chestnut tree. When I wanted a solution to some kind of difficulty that I was experiencing, I would sit under the oak tree and present my problem. I was always convinced that the tree would pour the solution into my head from the leaves above me because it never seemed to let me down.

If I wanted comfort, I would sit amongst the roots of a chestnut tree growing next to a stream. I felt its comforting and protective branches above my head. I would then imagine pouring my cares and woes into the stream and feel them flowing away from me.

I have used similar visualisations with my clients, based on those early childhood experiences, with excellent results. Now, if I am in the country, I love to sit relaxing under a tree and simply be aware of the strength of the tree in my back, the roots going deep into the earth and the protective branches above me.

We need a balance of the awareness of our rootedness in the earth and the energy of spirit to attain a true harmony in our lives. Our world is formed by the duality of form and spirit, the manifest and the unmanifest. It is as if we live our lives with a foot in two worlds, the physical and the spiritual.

This is a meditation for balancing these two opposing yet harmonising energies, a way in which you can centre yourself.

Centering

Relax down into a nice quiet place deep within you ... Let go ... Now imagine you are sitting beneath a tree with your back against the bark ... Visualise the roots of the tree going deep within the earth drawing up nourishment from its tap roots ... Now imagine there is a root or grounding cord growing downwards from your spine ... as if your spine is extending downwards and entering the earth ... going down and down into the earth ... even further down than the roots of the tree ... until it seems to rest in a place where the earth stores its nourishing energy ... It is a warm, red-brown energy ... With your in-breath draw it up through your tap root – your grounding cord ... Up and up, with the power of your intention ... Up into your body, filling your body completely up to the level of your waist ... Be aware of the warm, nourishing energy of Mother Earth ... It feels good ... You feel grounded in her love and care ...

Still maintaining that loving connection with Mother Earth ... Become aware of a beam of sunlight pouring down from a gap in the leaves above you and shining on the top of your head ... Be aware of the warm glow on your head ... And with your out-breath draw the Sun's golden light through the top of your head into your body down to the level of your waist ...

As you breathe in, you are drawing energy up from Mother Earth and as you breathe out you are drawing energy in from Father Sun ... Be aware of the two different energies in your body ... The warm, nourishing, rich, red-brown energy from the earth and the light, bouncing, golden spiritual energy from the sun ...

Feel your self balancing and centering ... Feel the harmony of these two opposing yet harmonising energies ... The Yin and Yang ... Light and Dark ... Male and Female ... Total balance ... You are perfectly balanced between Heaven and Earth ...

Enjoy this harmony for a while until you return your awareness to the place where you are relaxing ... When you are ready, gently open your eyes ...

By becoming grounded and centred, we can stay balanced while the world constantly changes around us. A tree stands upright and strong drawing nutrition from the earth and energy from the sun. Like a tree, we can remain rooted in our personal connection to the earth and reach and grow into the energy of spirit. We can be beautifully poised between Heaven and Earth receiving the gifts that both are offering to us.

16 *The Secret Garden*

Since I was very young, one of my favourite children's stories has been "The Secret Garden" written by Frances Hodgson Burnett. I still read the book and I also have a video of a film that was made in 1949 that I watch from time to time.

It is a beautiful story that can be seen as an allegory of our own journey of healing to find the stillness within ourselves. I will give you a brief synopsis of the story but please consider reading or rereading it for yourself.

After losing her parents in a cholera epidemic, Mary Lennox, a wilful and stubborn child (we might call her 'a little madam'), is sent to her widowed uncle's foreboding estate on the bleak Yorkshire Moors. Her uncle is a hunchback, an unhappy man who is bitter at the grief that life has caused him.

Mary meets her match in her crippled cousin, Colin, who is kept hidden from the world and makes his presence felt by throwing the most horrendous tantrums. He is convinced he will either grow up to be a hunchback like his father or that he will die young. Mary also befriends a local lad, Dickon, who is a totally different sort of child altogether. He is a simple country lad who has a magical affinity for animals and is in tune with the rhythms of nature. He speaks to animals in their language and has a 'green thumb' when it comes to growing things.

Mary and Dickon find a secret garden on the estate that had been locked up for many years following a tragic accident in which her uncle's wife was killed by a falling branch. Colin was born prematurely just before she died.

Dickon helps Mary to transform the abandoned garden into a wonderful sanctuary for the three children. The transformation of the secret garden; the mystery and beauty they find there has an incredibly healing effect on Mary and Colin. Colin finds an enthusiasm for life and walks for the first time in the garden. Mary discovers the magic of nature and finds she truly is a love-able, compassionate and attractive child.

All three children find an unsurpassable joy and a new aware-ness of life in their secret place. They find the magical garden of wisdom that lives within each of us.

The joy of the children also ultimately transforms the deep sor-row of Mary's uncle. The beloved garden gives them all the gift of happiness and healing. It also delivers them from the haunting grip of the past.

When we go inside to our own very special and magical garden of wisdom, we can be transformed and healed in the same way as Mary and Colin. We may not be crippled like Colin or hiding our sadness behind belligerent behaviour like Mary did, but we can transform our negative beliefs, heal our inner child and find inner peace and happiness within ourselves.

There is so much transformative work we can do in medita-tion. An invaluable visualisation to develop is finding your safe place. In the meditations later on in this book, you will be able to go into your safe place to meet aspects of yourself such as your intuition and your Higher Self.

Your safe place within could be a secret garden like the one in the story or somewhere else in nature. It may be a cave or even at the bottom of the sea. It may be in a cosy room or even a castle if you would feel safe there.

Finding Your Safe Place

Allow yourself to drift and float down deeper and deeper relaxed ... Imagine you are at the top of a beautiful, golden spiral staircase ... At the bottom of this staircase is your spe-cial safe place ... your inner sanctuary ... With each step you go down you go deeper and deeper into relaxation ...

Down and down ... deeper and deeper ...

Your inner sanctuary may be a secret garden ... on top of a mountain ... on a sandy beach ... in a park ... a clearing in a forest ... a log cabin in the hills ... but wherever it is, it's totally and completely safe ...

Allow it to be whatever it is ... Try not to censor your image ...

Have a good look around your safe place ... Explore ... What are the sounds, sights and smells in your safe place? ... How do you feel ... Are there any changes you would like to make here? ... Would you like to build a shelter? You can, you know ... It is your place ...

Relax in your safe place for a while ... or perhaps you would like to have fun, to sing, dance or play ... to celebrate having found your inner sanctuary ...

And when you are ready, gently open your eyes.

Your safe place may change from time to time or you may spontaneously add things to it. Trust your inner processes.

My first safe place, as you may imagine, was a secret garden with fragrant flowers in the flower beds, vines covering the stone walls and a gushing fountain. Now I have a little log cabin high up in the mountains overlooking forests and beautiful green valleys. Sometimes, I sit inside in front of a log fire in the cabin and at other times I sit on the porch outside. It has developed quite a bit over the years. If you have a building in your safe place, you can add on as many rooms or extensions as you wish. You will not need planning permission!

When you are really familiar with your safe place, you can enter into it simply by closing your eyes and desiring to be there. A safe haven from all the distractions of the world.

17 Intuition and Creativity

We are taught, from a very early age, that reason and logic are the tools that we should use to gain clarity and direction in our lives. We are encouraged to mistrust feelings, abstract thought and intuition.

Research has shown logic and reason to be functions of the left brain hemisphere and intuition, abstract thought and inspiration to be functions of the right. Also the left brain controls the function of the right side of the body and the right brain the left. It is interesting to consider that most of us are coerced into using our right hand for writing whatever our natural inclination may be. Perhaps this constant stimulation of the left brain is further encouragement to those faculties of logic and reason.

If we think of this in terms of energies, we can see a duality or polarity between the right and left sides of our brain; like Alternating Current (AC) and Direct Current (DC). Eastern philosophies have the concept of Yin, which is the feminine receptive energy and Yang, the masculine active energy. It is these two opposing yet harmonising energies which hold the universe together. The right-brain is the yin, feminine energy within us and the left-brain is the yang, masculine energy. We all, whether male or female, have these two energies within us.

Shakti Gawain in her book "Living in the Light", gives a great analogy to illustrate how these energies operate in our lives. She suggests thinking about the feminine intuitive energy as a road map with all the directions of how to get from A to B. The male energy is the vehicle with which you actually get to where you want to go. They are interdependent.

Our feminine energy is the creative thought and our masculine energy is the creative act. We need the masculine energy to manifest our creativity in the world. We need our feminine energy to give our actions purpose and direction. Remember, this process goes on within all of us, male or female.

As I said in Chapter Fourteen, the fourth kind of awareness comes into our conscious in the form of hunches, gut feelings, inspiration and a deep knowing. It is the "Ah-ha!" factor. This is our intuition, our feminine receptive energy. Trusting your intuition means being true to yourself, having the courage sometimes to take risks, trying new things because they **feel** so right.

Let us do a meditation where you can allow your intuitive feminine energy to take form so that you may communicate with her directly.

Meeting Your Intuition

Relax your mind and body ... let go of all the distractions of the day ... and drift into gentle relaxation ... Now visualise yourself in your safe place ...

Take in all the sights and sounds and smells of your safe place ... enjoy being there ...

Your intuitive feminine aspect is going to take form ... She may appear as a beautiful queen or a very old wise woman ... She may be a wood nymph or a priestess ... Allow her to be whatever she wishes to appear as at this time ...

Welcome her into your special place ... and invite her to sit with you ... If you don't get a clear image, that's okay ... just get a sense of her presence ...

If you wish to ask her for any guidance on any aspect of your life, do so now ... and remain open to any communication she may give you ... It may be transmitted from the form of her in front of you or it may be communicated by a voice within you ... your inner ear ...

When you feel complete with this communication, thank

her and say Goodbye ... just for now ...

Stay a while in your safe place to reflect on the experience of meeting with your Intuition ... on the guidance you may have received ...

And gently bring your awareness back to the room where you are relaxing ... and in your own time, open your eyes ...

You can do this visualisation as many times as you wish. As you learn to recognise the voice of your intuition, you will find you will be able to contact that wise aspect of your self, simply by turning your attention inwards and asking that still voice within.

When we have the courage to follow the course of our intuition, the manifested result will be increased creativity. It is as natural and sure as the dawn following the night.

So what actually is creativity? Let us return to the concept of male and female energies. Whereas the female energy or intuition provides us with the creative impetus; the inspiration, the male energy is the act of creation itself. It is the male energy which will manifest our dreams and inspirations; will put them into the world.

Creativity, in the broadest sense, is not just producing works of art or inspiring music. It is the ability to create one's own reality from within.

Creativity is also being fully in the present moment. Watch a small child painting. They are totally engrossed in what they are doing without any worries about what the end product is going to be. They use the colours boldly and fill the whole page. They paint for the joy of actually painting. The sad thing is when they become a part of an educational system which is bound up with the concepts of competition and achievement, their creativity may become stifled. They may paint a picture in order to gain approval or to be the best in the class.

There is a universal creative energy and our access to this is our birthright. We have inherited it simply by being born. Our intuition can lead us to ways to channel this energy. To understand what I mean by channel in this context, it is useful to use the analogy of an electrical wire which is not functional in itself but when electricity is passed through it, it channels energy to some purpose. Likewise, when we channel the creative energy of

the universe, we flow with that energy and can create or transform our environment in some way. We can regain the joy of creativity we once had as young children.

We all have the equal capacity to channel this creative force.
The only difficulty sometimes is to clear the fear, doubt and lack
of belief in ourselves that may block our conduits. I am sure that
most of us can recall a time when we desired to be creative in
some way but those negative voices popped up saying thing like
"You can't draw" or "You cannot sing" or "You will make a fool
of yourself". These doubts may have stopped the creative impulse
from being realised.

We may have been fed these negative beliefs in our abilities
from very early on from authority figures such as parents, teachers or even priests. As with all negative beliefs, it is important to
realise those voices are not us. By challenging those beliefs, we
can start to unclutter our creative channel.

Let us do a visualisation to discover and overcome any blocks
that are cluttering up your creative channel.

The Path of Creativity

Relax and deepen yourself ... Allow any thoughts to become
still ... Let go ... Take a deep breath and as you breathe out
allow every muscle in your body to completely relax ...

Now imagine you are walking along a path in a forest ...
See the bracken and ferns which line the path ... Smell the
wonderful scent of pine trees and feel the springy, mossy
ground beneath your feet ...

This is your path of creativity ... and as you walk along
this path, you will meet all those people who have imposed
upon you any limitations about your creativity ... As you
meet each one, you realise how you have taken on their
views as your own ... Maybe your parents with their expectations of something that was not really you ... Maybe
teachers who said you were stupid or not good enough ...
There may be school friends or work colleagues who made
fun of your creative ideas ... and others ...

Release the ideas they imposed on you as they pass you by on your path of creativity ... Release them as they now release you ... They may once have had your best interests at heart ... but now their views just hold you back ... You have no need of them ... none at all ... Let them go ...

Finally meet a mirror image of yourself on the path ... because surely there must have been plenty of times in your life when you yourself have put limitations on your own creativity ... As with all the others ... release this image of yourself ... with any last vestiges of limiting views that you may still hold about your creativity ...

And continue walking down your path of creativity until you come to a clearing in the forest ...

You are alone ... in this space affirm to yourself that you can now become a channel for the creative energy of the universe. If you wish, visualise in this space, what you wish to create in your life ... Know you deserve it ... You CAN do it. You really can.

And in your own time, bring your awareness back, become fully present in your body and gently open your eyes.

18 *Your Higher Self*

To begin this chapter, I will tell you about how a friend of mine found his faith in his Higher Power. I find the story very inspirational. I hope you do too.

David is a member of Alcoholics Anonymous and has been in recovery for five years. He did not come from any kind of religious background and, in fact, considered himself to be an agnostic. However, he wanted to work the twelve step programme as he knew from many others in the fellowship that it really worked.

The first three steps consist of firstly, admitting you are powerless in the situation that you find yourself in. Secondly, you acknowledge there exists a Higher Power than yourself and thirdly you hand over your problem, addiction, etc to that Higher Power. Alcoholics Anonymous stress that 'Higher Power' is whatever is meaningful for you. They are totally non-sectarian.

David could easily admit he was powerless but the issue of the Higher Power was another matter. He was determined not to be daunted by this and he went through the motions of the first three steps "as if" there was a Higher Power. It was a matter of "If anything is there, here it is - I hand it over because I cannot cope with it any more". And it worked.

He followed the twelve step programme successfully and has rebuilt his life in a most wonderful way. David discovered by "going through the motions" that there really **is** a Higher Power. He says he still does not understand what it is but he just knows **something** is there. He does not feel that it is important to understand it and I guess it's not.

Many times, when I am in bed at night preparing myself for sleep, I hand over to my Higher Power whatever loose ends of cares and worries I may still have left over from the day. Until I heard David's story, I felt my ability to do this may have been because of a strength of faith I have been developing over many years. What was so inspirational to me was that he had done it the other way round, taken the short-cut as it were and arrived at the same place as myself.

Many people (myself once included) balk at the word 'God'. It may hold many connotations of dogma, creed and concepts of original sin with all the guilt trips they entail. You may call that Higher Power the 'Power of the Universe', the 'Source', 'Divine Intelligence', 'Higher Power' or whatever else you may feel more comfortable with. As they say, "A rose is a rose by any other name".

Spirituality is a much broader concept than religion. It rests much more on personal experience and can be felt by witnessing the beauty of nature, listening to inspiring music or being with loved ones. It means trusting your intuition, being open to new things, allowing yourself to love and be loved, learning the lessons your experiences offer you and recognising that there is a power greater than your own in the world. This can lead you out of isolation and into a feeling of belonging to the whole family of humanity.

The personal contact with our Higher Power is what I refer to as our Higher Self. Our Higher Self is our highest octave of being, our essential spiritual Self. It provides the divine spark which ignites our life. It is that constant guiding presence within and around us which is totally loving, strong and wise. It is the bridge between our consciousness and that Higher Power. It is also the bridge that connects us to the human family.

A couple of years ago, I watched a very interesting television programme about a conference being held with some very eminent participants. It was on the functioning of the brain. All the world's leading neuro-physicists and, interestingly, enough all the world's leading theologians and philosophers were there in attendance. The Dalai Lama, the Pope, a glittering array of cardinals and many more were there.

For many years, up until that time, the neuro-physicists had been content with the model of the computer to rationalise the brain's function. This model made no room for a higher consciousness. However, eventually they perceived a fundamental flaw in their theory. If the brain was a computer, who was operating it? With all their extensive research they could not find a physiological answer to this problem. The theologians and philosophers sat at the conference while the scientists conceded that the only satisfactory explanation was that there must be a soul that was running the programme. It must have been quite an exciting moment for them all. Finally they were on the same side of the fence.

Think of developing your relationship with your Higher Self as a partnership because actually you both need each other. You need the guidance and nurturing your Higher Self can offer you and your Higher Self needs you to be its organ of awareness. Without you becoming fully conscious, your Higher Self cannot manifest its light, love and wisdom in the world.

If you find the concept of a Higher Self difficult to grasp, just experiment with assuming there is a loving, powerful presence within you and around you. Like David, try acting "as if" it is there. If you cannot believe or feel the love that your Higher Self has for you, pretend that you can. Imagine the love to be greater than you have felt extended to you before, that it is nurturing you, protecting and guiding you.

Your imagination can serve as a doorway into the inner world of love you hold deep within the centre of your being. This wonderful energy of love can heal your life and help to transform our planet. So allow yourself to feel the love within you and around you. Love is the energy that holds the universe together.

Here is a meditation to help you feel and recognise the presence of your Higher Self.

Higher Self

Relax and let go ... Relax your consciousness into a deep place within you ...

Now just imagine there is a powerful presence within you

... It has always been there ... loving and nurturing you but now you choose to become conscious of this presence ...

Now ask your Higher Self to give you some kind of signal ... a feeling or physical sensation that you can recognise it by ... so that you can KNOW there ... It may be a tingling in your feet, a tickle in your nose, a warmth around your shoulders ... You may see a colour or an image ...

If you do not feel or see anything right now, be patient ... Keep asking your Higher Self for that sign ... You will receive it because you have asked ... Just feel the love ... Let it in to your awareness ... Let it in and surrender to its love ... its love is always extending and expanding ... so simply surrender to its love ....

And when you feel ready, gently open your eyes ...

Repeat this meditation until you have a clear signal. Once you have it, call on your Higher Self from time to time and simply practise surrendering to its love.

Surrender does not mean giving up our responsibilities. It means trusting more. Those voids inside that we may have tried to fill with other people or short-lived pleasures, we can allow to be filled with light. It is not some lofty, mystical concept. It can be a very solid reality. If we trust our true selves (for that is what our Higher Self is), then we can trust in life's processes more and develop more meaningful relationships with other people.

We can also make our lives more fun and exciting. We can trust that it is okay to play, to be joyful, to love and be loved. The more we experience, acknowledge the presence of that Higher Power within us, the more we will recognise the same presence behind every pair of eyes we see. Then the miracles really start happening in our lives!

I believe the fusion or blending of our consciousness with our Higher Selves, the sacred marriage of form with spirit, is what the ancients called enlightenment. The journey to self-awareness is the fine balancing of the self with the Self.

Our Higher Self knows and understands everything about us, all our problems and difficulties, all our creativity and potentiality so in tapping into that wisdom we can transcend our limitations and apparent difficulties. We need never feel lonely again.

We spend so much of our lives looking for fulfilment out there and yet it is right here within us. There is an old Hindu fable about the gods deciding where to hide man's divine spark. One thought the bottom of the sea would be a good place, another the top of a mountain. These were decided against as they thought people were bound to find it there. They eventually decided if they were to place it **inside** us, it would be the last place we would look.

How true. However, it is there within us and all we have to do is look.

This is a meditation during which you can look within to your safe place and meet your Higher Self.

Meeting Your Higher Self

Relax and let go ... allow yourself to drift into gentle relaxation ...

Now find yourself in your safe place ... Use all your senses to make the place come alive for you ...

Now allow your Higher Self to take form and join you in your safe place ... It may take on human form, or appear as a sphere of light ... or you may simply sense its loving presence ...

Welcome it and feel its love extending towards you ...

Greet it in whatever way seems appropriate ... Perhaps, you could ask it if it would like you to call it by a name ...

If you would like to ask for any guidance, do so now ...

It has a gift for you but before you may receive the gift, there is something you must give up ... Maybe it is one of your resistances, self-doubt, or fears no longer relevant to you now ... What are you prepared to give up in order to receive your gift? ...

Hand it over to your Higher Self ...

Now receive your gift ... It may be in the form of an object, a symbol, a colour or even a word ...What is your gift? If you do not understand its meaning, ask your Higher Self ...

Thank it for the gift ... Also thank it for the love and

protection that it has extended towards you throughout your life and, indeed, throughout your many lifetimes ...

Now allow it to embrace you with that love and protection ... If it has appeared in human form, allow it to put their arms around you and hold you tight ... If it is a sphere of light, allow its light to enfold you ... or just feel its loving embrace ...

Surrender to its love ... and rest a while before you gently bring yourself back to your usual waking state and physical life ...

When I did this meditation a few years ago, my Higher Self introduced itself as Aurora. It has been very beneficial to me to have that name to call on when I need to feel its protection or receive guidance. I recognise its presence by a warmth around my shoulders and it feels so comforting.

In Chapter Six we looked at many ways with which you can create a positive future. In the same way that our Higher Self is our highest octave of being, co-creation is the highest octave of creation. When we allow our Higher Self to assist us in creating our reality, we bring in what Lazaris calls "the energy of together".

Whatever is created through a partnership with the Higher Self will be done with greater ease and success. With their guidance you can reach beyond your usual expectations and aspirations.

To be a co-creator, simply call on your Higher Self to be with you in your meditations, your reprogramming or whatever other technique you may be using and be open to their guidance.

Whenever I am going through a period where I am processing a lot of stuff, I call on my Higher Self while I prepare myself for sleep and request they assist my unconscious to make the adjustments necessary for my growth and development. Whenever I do this, I have the most amazing dreams so I know **something** is happening.

Part Three: Staying Centred

19 Getting Out of Your Own Way

However much inner work we do, whether it is meditating, affirmations or processing and reprogramming, our lives are constantly changing and fluctuating. Change brings us new challenges and allows for growth, development and progress if we remain open and flexible to be able to flow with those changes. Change is a natural law of life. I guess one of the biggest challenges it can present us with is how to stay centred within ourselves as we grow in an ever-changing world.

Very often while I am working with someone in therapy, I get the distinct impression they think I have all the answers. Because I have a whole armoury of techniques, meditations and exercises to empower one with the tools to discover self-awareness, they think that I have the whole thing sussed.

I feel the essential part of my job is to empower my clients with the knowledge that they each have all the answers they need within them. I am not comfortable with the role of guru and I very much doubt it would be beneficial for anyone for me to be in that role. So this is the time when I share with them something I may be working on at that time. It may be I am working on developing my Witness Self (which I will be talking about in the next chapter) or learning to express my anger appropriately.

When I do this, I often get a wide-eyed response as they say, "This work is an on-going thing. You are never really done, are you?". Of course, they are right. The journey to self-realisation is an on-going one. There is never a point when we can say, "Well, that's me done. I'm enlightened" and sit back on our spiritual laurels. We are in the school room of life and the school bell does not ring until we have fully learned the whole curriculum.

There will be times in our lives when we meet challenges from outside and inside. Sometimes we may be about to make positive changes in our lives and we get the feeling that something within is blocking our progress.

Do you ever get the feeling you are just getting in your own way, that things would probably go a lot smoother if you stopped putting obstacles in your way? It is a common complaint and I expect it happens to the best of us. Sometimes it may be due to the kind of resistances, negative beliefs or control issues we looked at in Part One but there could be another reason.

There may be an aspect of ourselves which is blocking us for a good reason. It may no longer be relevant but it was once. It could be an aspect of yourself which you created to help you in some way; to protect you from taking on too much or from getting hurt. It is not necessarily something which has been there since childhood (although it may well have been). It may have just been a month ago when you were made redundant or were jilted by a lover. It may be still in operation simply because it has not been told it is not needed anymore.

When you feel this may be the case, here is a visualisation you can use to clear that obstacle.

Overcoming Obstacles

Relax and deepen yourself ... Allow your thoughts to slow down ... and once again enter into your safe place ...

Reflect for a while on the situation in which you feel blocked ...

Now invite into your safe place the aspect of yourself which is blocking you in that area of your life ... Allow it to take form ... It may appear in human form, as an animal, a little gremlin, or even a younger version of yourself ... Accept whatever form it wishes to appear to you ...

If you wish to have your Higher Self present to help you, invite it also ...

Realise the aspect that is blocking you is trying to help you in some way ... even though it may be a bit misguided at this time ... so ask it how it thinks it is helping you ...

Be forgiving in your attitude with this aspect of yourself ... and thank it for trying to help but assure it you really do have other ways of doing things now ... and it can help you in some other way ...

Come to some kind of agreement on this ... If you have your Higher Self present, it may be able to give some guidance on how an agreement may be reached ...

When you feel you have reached a satisfactory arrangement, allow the image of that aspect of yourself to fade from your mind's eye ... thank your Higher Self for its help ... and gently bring your awareness back to your body ... flex your hands and fingers and gently open your eyes ...

This is a very useful visualisation technique to use for getting out of your own way. I used it a few years ago when I was first thinking about doing workshops.

Up until then, I had only worked as a one-to-one therapist. I was really keen to do the workshops but I found myself putting obstacles in the way, finding all sorts of excuses to put it off. I finally realised I must be blocking myself in some way. In the visualisation, the aspect blocking me appeared as a funny little gremlin. When I asked how he was trying to help, he told me he did not want me to feel bad if I failed at the venture and also he was not sure I could handle the extra workload.

I assured the little creature I was capable of doing the work and was ready to take on the challenge. We came to an agreement that it could help me to make sure I did not take on too much. The day after I did this, I was able to plan a short series of workshops which went really well and I gained the confidence to go on to do more. I now find workshops a very fulfilling part of my life.

Another excellent way I have found to help me to stay out of my own way is the one I mentioned briefly in the previous chapter. It is the third step of the Twelve Step Programme, handing over an issue that you know that you cannot handle to your Higher Power. It is giving up control.

Sometimes, when I am worried about something I feel my

intellect flexing itself and trying to take control. I start to analyse the situation so much I almost get a headache. For me, it is mainly my head that gets in the way. After a few mental gymnastics, I realise it is not the way to find a solution.

I talk to my Higher Self as if I was talking to a friend except that this friend is the wisest of all. I tell them the whole situation and request their help and hand the whole thing over to them.

I may receive some guidance right there and then with my inner ear but very often it will come within the next few days in all sorts of ways. I may chance to pick up a book and open it at a page with the insight I needed in the words right there in front of me. It may be that I run into a friend that I have not seen for ages and they offer the help I need or I may overhear a chance remark that somehow gives me a clue to finding the solution.

I believe that my Higher Self will be able to use all kinds of ways to supply me with the solution to my problem if I stay open and receptive and of course stay out of my own way.

As I said earlier, our growth is an on-going process. It is necessary to remind ourselves of this because we can get disheartened at times when we find ourselves in a situation where we feel powerless or depressed. I have said it myself when I have been a bit down, "Well, how far have I really come if I can get depressed about **that**" or if I feel a bit of sadness or regret coming up about a past relationship, "I thought I had dealt with that issue".

When I realise that I have started to beat up on myself in this way, I stop and think about the new lesson being presented to me, the new opportunity for growth I am being given. This new opportunity does not deny all the work I have already done. There may be just the last vestiges of an unresolved issue that finally I have the chance to lay to rest.

This way we can gladly take on the challenges of each new situation. When something happens in our lives which throws us off balance, we have the choice as to whether we look at what we can learn from the situation about ourselves, other people or life, or whether we simply suffer what life has dealt us.

When we make the choice to see what life is trying to teach us, we step out of the victim role and onto the path of the spiritual adventurer.

We learn the lessons and move on, clearing the obstacles to our growth as we go. Sometimes we may cry, sometimes we laugh, dance and sing but if we learn to stay out of our own way we will be ever moving forward on our journey. We find our next step from this one.

20 Non-attachment and the Witness Self

Whenever we attach our happiness to the behaviour of others and desired outcomes, we will be constantly at the mercy of our emotions. When that person does not react the way we want them to (or how we think they should) or things do not turn out the way we want them to, we will become unhappy. We may get angry, sad or resentful. Our perception can be so easily clouded by our emotional moods.

If we are attached to outcomes, we will experience fear and anxiety at waiting to see how things are going to turn out. We cannot be truly at peace and we certainly cannot enjoy being fully in the present moment while we are caught up in anxieties about the future.

If we feel we can only be truly happy when we **have** something or someone, we will always find that when we have the desired outcome there will be another goal that we will need to pursue. It will be like chasing the illusive rainbow - always just out of reach. Happiness that depends on anything outside yourself cannot last but happiness that is found within yourself, within your personal experience of life, is constantly being renewed.

There is nothing wrong in having things or even desiring them. The issue is what emotional attachment we have around those things; have we invested too much of ourselves in that desire.

Non-attachment does not mean being detached from the world. It just means letting loose your grip on things and people. It means being flexible, seeing things as they are and accepting the lessons in the experiences our lives are constantly offering us. When we are rigid in our outlook, we block out a lot of those new experiences.

The first step out of this rut is to be aware of what we are doing. When we are in a situation where we realise we are in an emotional web of our own making, we can step back and view the situation from a wider perspective. We will be more able to see the range of choices. We will be able to see, for instance, that we have the choice to drown our sorrows in alcohol, but we could choose to look within to our inner resources to find a solution, or we could ask for help.

If we allow ourselves to simply observe or witness our situation, we may be able to lighten up and see our way through much more easily. We may even see the funny side to it all. Remember, "Angels fly because they take themselves lightly"? One day I'm going to have it embroidered in large letters, framed and mounted on my bedroom wall!

I'll give you an experience to illustrate how developing the Witness Self can help you to detach from the emotions that can reel you in like a fish on a line.

I spent a week on my own in Greece meditating, writing, reading and generally recharging my batteries. It was a wonderful retreat.

The day after spending an idyllic day on the Isle of Symi, I went down to the village to have some lunch. I was sitting at a table writing my journal and some fellow tourists sat at the table next to me. I felt myself go into a 'better than'. I do not know whether it was because of what they were wearing, what they were talking about or whatever but I felt some kind of arrogance coming up inside of me. It is not an emotion I feel often and so my instant reaction was to beat up on myself up for feeling it. However, I stopped myself and simply observed what was happening within me. I did not let the emotion reel me in.

I ended up feeling very amused at the utter stupidity of my negative ego for feeling superior and it was very difficult not to let out a little giggle at its antics. It very soon passed and I was at peace again. I let it go.

Before I started to develop my Witness Self, if this had happened I would have spent much time castigating myself for feeling such a base emotion. Very likely my whole afternoon would have been spoiled by my attachment to the significance of the situation; how, after all my meditations the day before, I could sink so low as to be arrogant. As it was, it only took a few minutes to feel and subsequently release the emotion.

As human beings we have the wonderful capacity to feel emotions such as love, compassion, altruism and joy but we also have the capacity to feel hate, anger, arrogance and sadness. They are all part of our emotional repertoire.

Being witness to the experience of our emotions is not denying or repressing them. It does not stop us from feeling them. It means recognising that we are so much more than our emotions. It can give us a frame of reference.

As I said in Chapter Fourteen, we flit from one emotion to another constantly. Behind all our emotions is our awareness, the 'I am'. When you are experiencing anger, for instance, try saying to yourself, "I am aware of feeling anger" rather than "I am angry". There is a subtle but important difference because it is not really the whole of you that is angry, just a piece of you. It is only an emotion that shows you in which way you are attached to the particular person, thing or situation. As you stay with your observation, you will find yourself moving out of the emotion and into another that may be lying behind the surface.

You can find your root emotion, the base line, by simply observing your emotions and asking yourself, for instance, "Why am I angry?". The answer may be, "Because, I am hurt." The answer to why you are hurt may be "Because, I feel rejected." When your final answer seems to be "Just because I am", you have probably found your root emotion especially if, whenever you do this exercise, your final answer is very often the same one.

By getting into the habit of doing this when I felt out of balance emotionally, I found that the emotion that it always seemed to come down to was the fear of abandonment. I realised whenever I got myself into an emotional whirlwind, this fear was always there whatever other emotions may be floating on top. It had probably been lurking in the background of my unconscious for most of my life. Recognising it when it surfaced helped me enormously, because I could prevent it from colouring my perceptions in potentially emotional predicaments (especially, as you can imagine, in relationship issues).

Now when it appears my reaction is: "Oh, it's you again, fear of abandonment. Haven't seen you in a while." The more I began to witness how it came up in my life and noticed the situations in which it seemed activated, the less power it had over me, or should I say, the less power I gave it. Now, on the rare occasion it surfaces, I notice that it has really lost its edge and rather than being the monster fear it was, it is rather a pipsqueak of an anxiety which really doesn't have much credence at all.

If you are a bit of a worrier, start to notice when you are indulging yourself. Be a witness to all the little knots you create to tie yourself up in and give yourself a time limit. Allow yourself, say, a whole ten minutes to do nothing but worry.

At the end of the ten minutes think about what you may have achieved in that time; how worry has served you and then let it go. Hand it over to your Higher Self, sort out some relevant affirmations, have a brainstorm on possible solutions or anything else which may be more constructive. Soon you will find it more and more difficult to sustain that ten minutes of worrying. You will just get bored with it.

The process of stepping back and looking for the bigger picture means you do not need to **become** your problems, emotions, inner conflicts and confusion because they are only a small part of the picture.

Have you ever seen those art books where they show details of a painting? When you see the whole painting you see the detail you have been given in context. Well, it is the same with your emotions. The emotions you have about a certain issue are like those details. When you get the wider perspective, you step back from the emotional detail and get a better idea of who you really are and what is going on; the complete picture.

21 Other Aspects of The Inner Journey

We have images constantly rising into our conscious minds in the form of ideas, dreams and through the wondrous world of imagination. These images are the ways in which the different parts of our psyche communicate with our conscious minds and in many ways these inner images determine the quality and direction of our lives.

By exploring and changing our inner worlds, we can begin to transform our outer world. It is an inner journey that leads us to a greater awareness of the multi-faceted jewel that we are.

We have already looked at many ways you can use to go within in order to clear the debris of old belief systems and other obstacles on your path, find refreshment in the stillness and communicate with your Intuition and Higher Self. Now let us look at some other aspects of ourselves that it would be beneficial to meet on the inner journey to wholeness.

In Chapter Nineteen, I gave you a visualisation whereby you could meet an aspect of yourself which was blocking your progress in some way. This particular visualisation can be used in many ways.

For instance, using the same format; going into your safe place and perhaps inviting your Higher Self to help you, you could invite the aspect of yourself which is responsible for giving you migraines or some other kind of health problem that is a recurring theme in your life. Ask it why you need that particular pattern and then ask it to release you from it, coming to some kind of arrangement if necessary. You may find that there is a valuable lesson to be learnt at the core of your problem.

Staying on the subject of health, another useful visualisation to do is to go into a Healing Room and meet your Inner Healer.

Meeting Your Inner Healer

Relax and deepen yourself ... Allow yourself to gently drift down deeper and deeper into a nice, quiet place inside ...

Now imagine you are walking down a long corridor ...Walk down this corridor until you come to a door marked 'Healing Room' ...When you come to your Healing Room, realise that within this room is all that you need for your healing ... whether it is emotional, physical or spiritual healing that you need ...

And when you are ready ... walk into the room ... Here in the room you meet your Inner Healer ... So greet them in which ever way feels appropriate ... There may be lots of shelves with different coloured medicines upon them ... Look around the room and see what you can discover ...

Now talk with your Inner Healer about what it is you want healed ... Is it a physical problem or is it an emotional healing that you need? ... Is it a deep sense of sorrow or grief that you want lifted? ... Whatever the issue is, talk with them about it ...

They may give you words of comfort or hands-on healing ... They may bathe you in light or choose one of the medicines from the shelves ... They may also give you advice on where you may find help in your everyday life ... Accept their healing in what ever form it takes ...

And stay awhile in your Healing Room and soak up the healing energy that is present ...There may be a comfortable chair or a bed for you to rest on ...

Rest for as long as you wish ...

Before you leave the Healing Room, your Inner Healer wants to give you a gift that symbolises the healing that you can take with you into your everyday life ... Accept this gift ... Ask the Healer what it means ... Then place it somewhere within your body ... so you can be aware of it in your usual waking reality ...

And when you are ready, leave the Healing Room knowing you can return at any time ... and gradually bring back your awareness to the room where you are relaxing ... and in your own time, gently open your eyes ...

Your Inner Healer is a very useful aspect of your self to get to know. It is an aspect of your unconscious that knows all there is to know about your body's needs and therefore can advise you on your self-healing process.

Your unconscious keeps your heart beating and blood pumping through your veins. It maintains the rhythm of your breathing and does a hundred thousand things your conscious mind is not even remotely aware of, every second of your life. The only importance of realising this is that you know you can trust your unconscious processes to do something that is beneficial, especially when it is given the proper stimulus to do so. This kind of inner work provides that stimulus.

Our true selves are beautiful, shining and powerful beings but we so often hide our light beneath layers of inferiority and assumed mediocrity. But underneath all these garments of negativity is our inner beauty. The more we peel away those layers, the more we allow ourselves to shine.

In our society, we can easily get fixated on getting the packaging right. By 'packaging' I mean the right clothes, car, house, job, image and life style. We are encouraged to do this by the whole media industry. They constantly give us the message that if we are beautiful or handsome, wear the right fragrance, 'delay the ageing process' and drive a prestigious car, we will be happy, able to attract the right mate and be fulfilled. And we so often fall into the trap, don't we?

At one time, Jane was a real jet-setter. She was (and still is) a very glamorous lady. She had the Porsche, her own company, beautiful expensive designer clothes - the lot. Her packaging was perfect. She was admired and envied by many people.

Then the recession hit hard. She lost her car, had to make people redundant and when I first met her, she was about to face insolvency and was suffering from depression. The 'packaging' was crumbling around her feet.

It was the impetus for Jane to look a little deeper into the meaning of her life. She realised that all the things she had used to prop her personality up with were flimsy and insubstantial. By embarking on an inner journey, she found the resources which would always be with her whatever the economic, social or emotional climate she may find herself in during her life.

Jane has subsequently rejoined the fast lane but those resources are still there within her awareness. She now says the recession was the best thing that could have happened because it gave her the opportunity to rebuild her life on a more solid foundation. She became aware of her inner beauty and she grew what I have come to call the 'magic two inches'.

So what are 'the magic two inches'? One of the most satisfying aspects of my job as a counsellor, is noticing how people seem to grow taller by about two, maybe three inches when they start to feel good about themselves and allow themselves to shine. It's a delightful phenomenon to be witness to. They start to look at the world head on and their whole posture reflects this. Their spine elongates, their head is held higher and their shoulders are back. Consequently, they do really seem to have grown.

Beauty is not a quality that is confined to women. The dictionary definition of beautiful is, "delighting the eye and ear; morally or intellectually impressive, charming". So men can be beautiful too.

Although it may be fun to play with the 'packaging', our inner beauty is not in the least bit affected by it. It also cannot be tarnished by age or deformity. It is not enhanced by the right cosmetics or the razor which is 'the best a man can get'. Our inner beauty just is.

It is an eternal light shining within us. We simply need to uncover it, let it radiate. When we do this, people will respond to us in a more profound way than when they are simply reacting to the package we have put together.

So how about acknowledging your inner beauty?

Finding Your Inner Beauty

Allow yourself to relax ... Just let go ... Breathing quietly and deeply, go within and be still ...

Now let yourself drift into your safe place ... and allow yourself to just be ...

Now allow your inner beauty to reveal itself before you ... See an image of yourself as the beautiful, powerful, serene and radiant being that you truly are ... See your inner light and love radiating outwards ... Bathe in that irridescent loveliness ... Acknowledge your inner beauty ... It is you ... Truly you ...

Greet it ... It has been waiting so long for you to notice it ... to notice the beautiful you ...

How do you feel seeing your inner beauty? ...

Affirm that you will take the recognition of your inner beauty into your life ... That you will let it shine out to everyone you meet ... The world wants you to shine ... It needs you to radiate your beautiful light to help to heal the denial of beauty ...

Embrace your inner beauty and allow it to dissolve itself into you ... Feel every cell in your body tingle with recognition ...

And whenever you feel ready, take a couple of deep breaths, become aware of the room and gently open your eyes ... and notice how you feel right now ...

You may want to do this visualisation when you feel yourself getting caught up in the 'packaging game' or perhaps when you feel that you may be hiding your light under a layer of 'not good enough'.

Another way to access information from the unconscious in order to gain greater understanding, is to go within the stillness and request that your unconscious give you a symbolic image relating to the issue you are dealing with. For instance, you could ask your unconscious mind to give you an image to symbolise what it is you need in order to develop more self-esteem or self-love. It may be that you want an image that can show you what is blocking you from receiving love, abundance, etc.

Accept the first image that appears and allow it to become clearer. When you have a clear enough image in your mind's eye, open your eyes and draw a picture of it. (Have your coloured pens at the ready for this exercise.) When you have the picture of your image, make a note of the thoughts and feelings that came to you during the visualisation and also any subsequent insights which may have come up as a result of putting it on paper.

Allow yourself to experiment on your inner journey. Take the suggestions in this book and put them into practise in your own unique way. You will probably come up with better ones than I have ever thought of.

Part Four: Love

22 *Love, the Only Reality*

What is love? It is a word that is used so often. We say that we love ice-cream and chocolate. We love to dance and when we feel a close and special connection to someone, we say that we are 'in love' with them. Because of all the intrigue and fascination as well as the confusion and bewilderment around this little word, Part Four is devoted to taking a deeper look at it.

I am just going to present my ideas and beliefs on love. I am not particularly attached to these beliefs as they are growing and developing all the time. But I hope that you may resonate with at least some of them or they will trigger your own ideas on love.

I would like first to clear up some of the misconceptions around the issue of love. The most common, I think, is feeling that you need someone or something to direct love to or to have a special person in your life to love you in order that you may be able to experience the feeling of love.

When we **allow** ourselves to feel the warm glow of love springing up from deep within us, we are 'in love'. Our Higher Self loves us unendingly and we can feel its love at any time we choose simply by being willing to bring it in to our awareness. And of course, that Higher Power, whatever we conceive it to be, loves us unconditionally. The only thing that can separate us from that love is the feeling that we may not worthy of it – nothing else.

When we say that we are in love, we may feel that it is only through that other person that we can experience that exquisite feeling; as if they have created it for us. But what we feel is

really a beautiful and loving aspect of ourselves that has been triggered off by our relationship with that person. That love has been
there all along, it just needed a trigger. We can 'trigger' that feeling through meditation and surrendering to the love that is within us and around us.

Some people may fear that they are not loveable or are not
capable of loving. The fear of being humiliated or rejected or our
own low self-esteem could be reasons why we may erroneously
come to this conclusion but we are all capable of loving and being
loved. We just need the willingness and perhaps a little courage to
dispense with that negative belief.

Underneath all the layers of our physical bodies, our personalities, egos, intellects and psyches, we are love. Love is at the core
of our being. It is our natural state of being. So if you think you
are unloveable or are unable to love, perhaps it would be beneficial to find out what your resistances are to allowing yourself to
love and be loved. There are many techniques that you can use to
do this. Many of those that I have already given you would be
well suited to this purpose.

We may also have some strange definitions about love that we
have inherited from our parents. For instance, we may have
learned that love is sacrifice from statements like, "Of course I
love you. Look what I have sacrificed for you." Or we may have
learned from our role models (usually our parents) that if you
love someone, you need to play the victim/martyr role. From
these erroneous definitions, love may seem to be self-denial, suffering or being a slave.

Think for a little while on what your definition of love is. Write
it down. What qualities does your definition have? How do you
think you have arrived at such a definition? After you have done
this, go into a reflective meditation as explained in Chapter
Thirteen using love as your focus. Just keep asking the question,
"What is Love?" and see what insights your inner wisdom supplies you with. Write this new definition down and compare it
with your original one.

Love is a pure energy that is within and around us and we all
have access to it. When we open our hearts, we can channel it
through us. I believe that love is the creative force of the universe
and there is an inexhaustible supply of it. Love supplies the

matrix that holds all matter together. Love is all there is; the only reality.

Love conquers fear, can heal our lives and can be expressed in thousands of different ways. There are many components to its expression such as trust, respect, caring, honesty, compassion and acceptance.

If we return to the concept of feminine and masculine energies (yin and yang), the state of being is feminine and the state of doing is masculine. You cannot have one without the other. Love requires the feminine and masculine functioning together in harmony. For love to manifest in the world means action – the **act** of loving.

For it to be able to flow freely though us and into the world with our actions, it needs to start with ourselves. Truly experiencing the energy of love means loving ourselves and then allowing that love to flow out towards others.

True self-love is not self-serving or generated from the ego. Until we love and accept ourselves, we cannot extend our love to others successfully. Self-love will open the doorway to a real sense of union with your Higher Self. You will not be able to receive the love of your Higher Self, Higher Power or another person until you love yourself. How else would you feel that you deserved it? How else could you **allow** yourself to be loved?

If you do not love yourself you will find great difficulty in believing that someone else could love you. You will find yourself in what I call the Groucho Marx syndrome. He came out with a great one-liner once when he said, "I wouldn't want to be a member of a club that would accept someone like me as a member". Recognise that feeling in the context of relationships? I certainly remember being caught up in that one in the past.

So do your affirmations, focus on all your positive attributes, be a good friend and be kind to yourself. Begin to love and accept yourself unconditionally. Pretty well all the exercises that I have given you already in this book are going to help you, at least in part, develop that essential self-love. They work. All you need to understand is that you are worth the trouble to actually do them. Remember that you cannot love another any more than you love yourself.

The main components of love are caring, respect and trust and, once these are present, giving will be the manifested result. We will look closer at these components but remember that they apply to self-love as well as the love we extend to others.

Caring is a genuine and honest concern for the well-being of others (and yourself). It is not being complacent about the lives of others. It is wanting to know more about them; what they are feeling. It is not taking people for granted or anticipating outcomes. If we truly care for someone, we desire to help them in whichever way is right for them; not in a way that just makes us feel good or is in any way interfering with their own development.

Respect is a vital ingredient of loving, whether it is self-respect or respect for others. We earn our self-respect by developing an appreciation of the way in which we handle our emotional well-being; the way we express our emotions appropriately and honestly.

Respecting others can be a stumbling block if what they are doing or saying is something that we do not like. However, what we can do is respect their right to do or say that and detach. It does not mean that we have to tolerate the behaviour that is directed towards us if it is unacceptable. Out of self-respect, we may have to deal with the situation in some way.

Respect means acceptance; allowing others to be who they are. It means not insisting that someone changes for our benefit. We all have our own paths to tread. It is wonderful that our paths may run in parallel with someone else's at times but we must respect that they have their own unique history, present and potential future.

Without trust, love cannot manifest fully in our relationships but trusting yourself must come first. It is only then that you will no longer need to be possessive or jealous and you can allow yourself to trust another. When you have learned to trust yourself, you will have also learned to let go, relax and trust in life's processes more.

For me, trust was a very big issue to overcome in my life. The resolution of this came with developing a close relationship with my Higher Self, having the courage to follow its guidance and allow its love and protection to come into my awareness. It was this that gave me the courage to begin to trust; to know that whatever happened, I could handle it. It was okay for me to share my vulnerability with certain people and I could trust my intuition to know who those 'certain people' were.

When the qualities of caring, respect and trust are present, we can be led to the act of loving itself which is **giving**. The giving may be tangible or intangible.

As far as giving to yourself is concerned, it means being kind to yourself. It means taking good care of your physical, emotional, mental and spiritual well-being. It is giving yourself the space sometimes just to be yourself. It is tuning in to what your needs are and doing what you can to fulfil them.

When you give to others, you don't have to spend a lot of money on an expensive gift in order to let them know that you love them. It really is the loving thought that counts. Sometimes, a postcard or even a scrap of paper with your sincere thoughts on it can touch someone's heart more than an expensive card, and a single rose to a lover can be so much more intimate than a whole bunch. Also, a sincere prayer for someone's well-being is a wonderful act of giving. You can give love as a thought or feeling.

Love can transform all negative thoughts and feelings when we raise them to the heart centre. To implement this kind of transformation, when I feel anger, for instance, I focus on where I can feel it in my body (it is usually in my stomach). Then I visualise a pink rosebud in the centre of my chest and as I breathe in I raise the anger in my stomach up to that rosebud. As I breathe out I imagine the rosebud opening and transforming the emotion into love.

This can be done as quickly as it takes to breathe in and breathe out. I have done it whilst I have been talking to someone and have noticed the quality of the energy between us change and lighten. I have done it while I am walking down the road if I am feeling nervous about something and very soon I feel myself calming down.

We can make the conscious decision to be a loving person. This does not necessarily mean that we will love everyone. Sometimes, we will encounter people that we do not love or even like too much but we can still be a loving person to that individual. We can still remain true to ourselves and respect that person's right to be that way and accept their path as distinct from our own.

If you make the decision to be a loving person, you allow the wonderful energy of love to flow through all that you do. You will lay aside judgements or criticisms and will discover the gift of loving acceptance that you can freely give to others as well as to yourself.

You will learn to be patient with yourself and others. You will acknowledge that it is alright to make mistakes. You will have the courage to trust without guarantees. When you are with someone with whom you want to become more intimate, you will be able to trust yourself and them enough to share your vulnerability as well as your strength.

As a loving person, every act of kindness and sincerity that you give will add more light to our world.

23 Love, The Antidote To Fear

Fear can be beneficial to us when it is operating to protect the physical body from harm. For instance, if a child was not taught, by experience or by their elders, to be afraid of fire or crossing the road without looking, they would constantly be in some kind of danger.

If we do not have a certain amount of fear in our everyday lives, we may recklessly go into situations that may imperil our well-being in some way. We may drive too fast, walk too close to the edge of a cliff or swim too far out of our depth, etc. This is part of our basic survival instinct and it would be better described as caution. This was fear's original and correct function in our consciousness.

Caution also provides a necessary constraint to our progress at times. Without caution, the positive aspect of fear, we may not slow down enough to see our direction clearly. We may make rash decisions in the heat of the moment or rush headlong into situations without due consideration. In this respect, fear can be an invaluable ally, a resource that can serve us well.

However, fear in any other aspect is a distortion of this primal function; a mutation. It is of our own creation but it can end up controlling us instead of us controlling it. It can become an unconscious monster; the minotaur in our labyrinth.

It is a shadow of reality that is created out of our forgetfulness and our distrust of ourselves. It is the unknown of our imagination. It is not real. It is merely an area of darkness that will disappear when the light of love and truth shines on it. Fear is the absence of and the longing for love.

Remember the story of The Beauty and The Beast? Think of that story as an allegory of how we conquer the beast of fear, our shadow, with the beauty of the essence of our being which is love. The beast is then transformed back to the prince that he really was all along. The fear is transformed back to the function it was always intended to be; serving us instead of paralysing us.

We all have that dark side; a shadow. The shadow is made up of denied fear; the unspoken, hidden, unknown fears. Darkness is only an area of ourselves that has not been exposed to the light. The more we deny that shadow within us, the more power we give to it.

Whatever we deny, we become more attached to. We cannot release it by rejecting it. Only by accepting it with love as a part of us, just as Beauty lovingly accepted the Beast, can we transform our fears back into the resource that they once were.

It really is a matter of loving and accepting ourselves – warts and all. (Yes, we are back to that again!) This is the key to conquering fear, taking our power back and making fear our servant once more. We need to be compassionate with ourselves; to accept our areas of ignorance and fear as a parent may lovingly accept the unruly behaviour of a young child.

Underneath any negative emotion is fear. It may be the fear of abandonment, rejection, humiliation, being wrong, etc. We may fear to love or to trust.

Whenever you are feeling ill at ease emotionally, it can be useful to ask yourself "What am I afraid of?" There will be a fear under there somewhere. Don't be vague about the fear. Be specific. See what comes up.

When you bring that dark area under the light of consciousness you are able to see it for what it is – merely a shadow pretending to be a bogeyman. You can then begin to understand it and put it to work for you.

There are times when you know exactly what the fear is and it is haunting you constantly. You fear losing your job or you fear that your husband/wife is having an affair, etc. Then you can go into a meditation and play your worst fears out; play them to the hilt. See the whole scenario as if it were a television drama or soap opera. If you possibly can, try to see the humour. Step out of yourself and see yourself go through the drama. This will get it out of your system as it were. Then the fear is no longer a denied one and will not be exerting as much power over you.

You will also probably see that you can handle it anyway; there are always solutions. Doing this will not make it happen. Your unconscious does not know the difference between imagination and reality so acting it out in your mind will seem as if it has happened anyway. Therefore it will not need to manifest it in your reality. It can be released.

Many times in our society, we feed fear more than we feed love. We give it power over our lives but we do have the choice to take that power back. Have you seen the film "Ghost-busters"? The slime that was lurking under the city in the sewers was like a collective shadow of fear that was being fed by the negativity of the city. It was conquered by love, hope and courage (with the help of the Statue of Liberty). It just melted away.

Fear relies on the past. When you transform the shadow beast, you will gain freedom from the past and will be able to create the future that you deserve.

It just takes willingness to let go of your fears. You may be hanging on to your fears because they serve you in some way. They may help you to avoid certain things that you do not want to do or feel that you are unable to face like intimacy or success. If you feel that you have a pay-off in hanging on to a fear, go into a meditation, imagine yourself in your safe place and allow that pay-off to take form and join you. Ask it what it is trying to do for you and release it in some way. It will be a similar meditation that I gave you in Chapter Nineteen.

Fear is not real. It is really just your imagination playing tricks on you the way shadows in a child's bedroom can look like monsters. Therefore, by using your imagination in positive ways such as visualisation, you can transform it from within. Maybe you could play out a fairy story in your mind such as the Beauty and the Beast. Imagine the monster that you have created and transform it with your love into the prince that will help you to live happily ever after.

As fear is also born out of forgetfulness, another way of dealing with fear is to ask yourself what it is that you have forgotten.

If you are fearful, it is simply that you have forgotten who you are. You have forgotten that you are a beautiful piece of all that is and as such are an integral part of the whole divine plan. You have forgotten that you are so much more than your emotions, your thoughts, your body and especially that you are so much more than your fears.

Sort yourself out an affirmation to remind yourself of this. Maybe something like, "I am a radiant, loving and serene child of the Universe", "I am a channel for universal love", or "I am allowing love to flow into my life". As soon as you remember that you are really a radiant and loving creator of your own reality, all fear will dissolve away.

Love is the ultimate antidote to fear. It is a much more powerful force than fear. Try this meditation for cleansing and transforming fear with love.

Cleansing Fear With Love

Sit with your back straight and your feet resting on the ground ... Allow yourself to drift into relaxation ... Breathing easily and deeply, allow each breath to take you deeper and deeper down into relaxation ...

Now become aware of where fear is in your body ... Where do you feel the sensation of fear? ... Is it in your solar plexus? ... in your back? ... Do you sense it in your neck? ... Locate it in your body ...

When you have located it, focus on it. Maybe you could give it a shape and colour so that it is tangible ...

Now imagine that there is an opening at the top of your head and through this opening is pouring a stream of golden light ... It is the light of the Love of your Higher Power ... The Love of the universe is pouring into your body through the top of your head ... Feel it filling your entire body ...

Feel it pouring into and around that area of fear ... It is dissolving it, transforming it into light and is carrying it out of your body ... through your feet and into the earth ...

Continue for a while being aware of this stream of light

and love cleansing your entire body of fear ...

Now imagine yourself experiencing a new and healthy vitality and energy that flows through your body and your mind ... Imagine yourself living your life without fear ... See yourself go through the routines of your day as a person without fear ... How does it feel? ... Notice how other people interact with you now ...

And when you feel ready, bring your awareness back to the room and gently open your eyes ...

I came across a great doggerel on the word 'fear' a little while ago which gives some idea of its meaning: Fantasised Expectation that Appears Real.

Fear will block us from taking positive steps forward in our lives. When I had just passed my driving test, I remember experiencing how fear wanted to drag me back to the past.

I had been so used to driving with the security of having my instructor there supporting and encouraging me, that going out on my own in a car that I was not used to was quite terrifying at first. Exciting but nonetheless terrifying. Everyone was saying, "You must go out in the car every day to get your confidence." I knew they were right but it was hard to motivate myself to do it.

One day, I was at home thinking about going through the ordeal of driving and I felt myself go into what was very much like a five-year old tizzy. I felt tearful and was saying to myself, "I wish everything would go back to the way it was when I couldn't drive. I don't like it." I almost stamped my feet! I allowed myself to go right into it and ended up laughing my head off. The laughter seemed to dissolve the fear into thin air.

Then I was able to think about what would take the apprehension out of driving alone. Somebody suggested having a teddy bear in the car sitting in the passenger seat but I decided to imagine my Guardian Angel sitting there. I figured they would be a lot more helpful in a crisis than a teddy! The trepidation very soon subsided.

All the obstacles that we may put in our way, all our limitations and resistances have their origins in fear. We have the choice whether we give it the power over us or not. Freedom from our creations of fear can enrich our lives so much.

We gain more confidence, self-esteem/love. We develop the courage to take risks; to go for it instead of being paralysed by the fear of failure or success. We learn to laugh at ourselves; to see the funny side of our predicaments instead of suffering the fear of humiliation. We are also free to form more loving, satisfying and fulfilling relationships instead of hiding behind our fear of rejection and abandonment.

We have the choice to walk out of the shadow of fear and into the light of love.

24 Relationships

This is the area in our lives that can be so full of minefields. Relationships are such a big challenge, aren't they? They can be the thing we want but also fear the most.

One of the reasons for this is that relationships will be the arena for unfinished business; they will drag it to the surface. If we do not recognise and take responsibility for the areas of our unconscious that we have not yet integrated and deal with them appropriately, we will project them onto our partner. We will blame them for making us unhappy or angry when really the emotions we are feeling may be going back to a time before we had even met them.

I'm sure there have been times when you have overreacted to a given situation. You have blown your stack at a triviality or you have witnessed someone else do it. When anyone reacts emotionally in a way that is over and above what the situation calls for, you can bet your bottom dollar that there is a buried emotion that has just been triggered off and is lighting the fuse.

If we have not resolved our fear of rejection that we have carried though from our childhood, we will view the relationship through the veil of our fear and perceive rejection where none is intended. If we have an unconscious fear of being dominated, we will see relationships as a power struggle. If we were brought up by a manipulative parent, we will suspect and fear manipulation from our partner and may end up being manipulative ourselves.

If we were abused as a child, whether mentally, physically or sexually, and have not released the emotions that constellated themselves around it, we will probably repeat the pattern of abuse in our relationships. Therefore, we may be unconsciously attracted to the person that will bring these things to the surface in order to release them.

Our relationships really are our mirrors. It is through them that we can see the beauty within ourselves, our incredible capacity for loving as well as our fears, doubts, negative beliefs and holding patterns of behaviour.

I once had a relationship in which my partner constantly judged and criticised me. He was always wrongly accusing me of all sorts of things and had an infuriating habit of telling me what I was thinking and feeling. Whenever I said that he was mistaken, he would say that I was just not in touch with it. However, when this was not going on, he appeared to be the most wonderful and loving person you could imagine. It was a very strange relationship which seemed to be held in a pattern of constantly swinging back and forth from heaven to hell.

I was constantly rejected but always went back for more until I decided that it was about time I learned the lesson that this relationship was trying to teach me. I knew that if I did not resolve it, I may continue the pattern of attracting criticism and judgement in another relationship and I had certainly had enough of that.

I realised that one of the main issues that this relationship was mirroring to me was the judgement and criticism I held against myself. I had often put myself down, and when anything went wrong I always blamed myself. I saw quite clearly that I had drawn just the right person into my life to exaggerate that part of me so much that I could finally release it from my unconscious as I rejected it from my life. I had been pushed to the victorious point of stepping out of being a victim of criticism and judgement wherever it came from.

I am truly grateful to him for that because it led me to develop a loving acceptance of myself. I no longer beat myself up with criticism or have anyone in my life that does it for me. Now, if I look at the people in my life, I see that I have only loving, caring and supportive people around me. What a different mirror!

There are so many other dynamics that go on within a relationship; one being that so often we are attracted to someone for the qualities that we really need to develop in ourselves.

This is why an introvert can be so attracted to an extrovert and vice versa. An introvert is someone who mainly directs their energies inwards towards their inner needs and an extrovert directs energy towards their outer needs. The introvert may need to achieve balance in their life by taking more care of their outer needs and the extrovert could well benefit by looking to their inner needs at times. The trouble is if this factor is ignored they will simply allow their partner to act out that trait for them.

The only path to an equal relationship is for both partners to work towards becoming whole in themselves; supporting each other in their development and growth, flowing with the changes that come about on the way and loving each other enough to drop the defences of blame, martyrdom, avoidance and judgement.

In Chapter Twenty Two, we looked at the components of love; caring, respect and trust. In a relationship there are also two more components that need to be present before love may manifest in giving (the act of love). They are intimacy and commitment.

I know at one time, the very sound of these words would strike terror into my heart and they do the same for many of us. A fear of intimacy can block us from giving and receiving love. That fear is usually synonymous with the fear of rejection or abandonment because of past broken promises, shattered illusions, etc.

Intimacy is a deeper level of caring for that other person; honestly and intensely caring for that person's well-being. It means listening to them so that you can learn more about them. It means never taking them for granted or predicting what they may say or do; having the humility to realise that things may be different with each new situation.

Intimacy also means being brave enough to allow yourself to be vulnerable with another. Your vulnerability can be such a precious gift to give to the one you love. I have always been an independent person. I was always the person that my friends came to for support. My shoulders were big enough for everyone to cry on. I used to think it was my role in life somehow.

The trouble was that I used to find it difficult, if not impossible, to return the favour of letting someone else offer their shoulder for me when I needed it. I remember the first time I plucked up the courage to let someone else know that I was vulnerable. It was scary! I was trembling like a leaf. However, they were so happy I had given them the chance to care for and support me. It is not an issue for me now and I have found as a result, my friendships and relationships have been at a much more profound and intimate level than they could have been before.

As for that other scary word, commitment, this can only be made after there has been built a strong foundation of caring, respect, trust and intimacy. It can not successfully come about before as it would be like building a house on shifting sand. It simply would not last.

Commitment does not just mean saying the words, "I love you". It means being there for someone no matter what. It also means taking responsibility with that other person for the interaction between them both. Both parties need to recognise they are each a hundred per cent responsible for their part in the interaction; for their thoughts, emotions and actions within the relationship. Commitment means an agreement that each of them will not 'dump' their emotional garbage on their partner and that they will help each other working through any problems that arise without apportioning blame or taking on guilt.

There are many things that can masquerade as love, such as neediness and our illusions about what love is. We may also be more in love with the 'package' than the person inside it. We need to separate these things from our reality; peel away the masks to see what is there.

It is important to separate neediness from love. Are you in the relationship for what you can get out of it? Are you more concerned with your own needs than with what you can give ? Would you not be able to cope without them? Are you avoiding facing your inner pain by hiding in a relationship? These issues can definitely bond two people together but it may have very little to do with love.

We all have needs and that is okay. It is also okay to ask for help with those needs but when we become powerless without that support, we stop growing as a person. We stifle our creativity and aliveness.

Traditionally, our society has always encouraged people to believe that the ultimate fulfilment for an individual (especially for women) is to be married and have children.

Many of us nowadays are questioning this and are finding fulfilment within ourselves in many different ways. In our relationships, we are working towards having equal partnerships without the strict delineation of roles of the traditional marriage. This is quite a breakaway and because of this, relationships can often seem like journeys without maps. We are like pioneers charting new territories; following our hearts and being guided by our intuition.

There are so many romantic illusions about love. They get fed to us from Hollywood and love songs. These illusions are not about love. They are fantasy that is fine for the movies, but we don't live like that. Love is a reality. In real terms, love means having the courage to trust and trust is not insisting on the kind of perfection we may see played out on the movie screen or hear about in a love song.

Some people just love to fall in love. They do not like staying in love; learning to care, respect and trust someone. That seems too heavy, and commitment – no way! The buzz you get from the adrenalin rush of 'falling in love' can be as addictive as a drug. It takes a certain amount of emotional maturity to **stay** in love with someone.

Of course there also may be the danger we may fall in love with the packaging rather than the person. This means that we love some**thing** rather than some**one**. It may be they are beautiful or handsome, successful or well-read. They may have been to the right workshops or know the right people. We may also feel we need to get our own packaging right before anyone can love us. This may not be as obvious and superficial as it sounds. It could be quite subtle.

If you are not in a relationship and feel you want to be in one take this thought and let it rumble around your head for a while. If you were really ready for a relationship, it would already be there for you in your life. Look within to find the parts of you that do not want it; fears and anxieties, doubts and denials. Do some spring-cleaning and when you have finished, someone will be there for you.

As with love, acceptance, trust and respect, relationships start with ourselves; having a good relationship with ourselves. All relationships with others are simply mirrors of this primary relationship.

This means listening to your needs and having the courage to ask for help sometimes. It means following your intuition and dealing with your emotions appropriately. It means lovingly accepting yourself on all levels of your being. As you build that relationship with yourself, so you will find that love will flow more easily into your life. You will open up a channel for love and your relationships will reflect a deeper level of intimacy and passion.

Each relationship is an opportunity to experience more love in your life and love is really the only thing that is important in each moment.

When you can look into another person's eyes and see the light within them; see their inner beauty shining out at you and know that you are seeing a beautiful reflection of yourself, your relationship can then become the most exquisitely joyous and intimate dance – the eternal Dance of Love.

25 Unconditional Love

Before we look at unconditional love, let us consider its opposite. Conditional love is putting restrictions on when or how we will love someone and if these conditions are not met, we withdraw our love. It is a case of, "I will only love you if you love me in return, tell me I am wonderful, agree with me, have the same interests, love my friends and family, do not love anyone else, say you will never leave me, are always open with me, tell me that you have never loved anyone as much as you love me, etc, etc." There are demands, restrictions and expectations that need to be met before the gift of love is given.

This kind of love is simply an illusion. It is not love at all. It is manipulation. I feel that when we channel the pure energy of love into ourselves and then attempt to use it in this way before we allow it to flow out to another, it does not remain pure. It becomes something less than love. It may become possessiveness, domination, neediness or sentimentality – cheap imitations of love.

Think honestly about any conditions or demands that you may have in place towards those close to you. Then consider whether they need to be in place. Are there any that you could fulfil yourself in some other way. Choose just one and commit yourself to letting it go within the next few days or so and maybe you could gradually work your way through the others. Also try to remember a time when you loved and/or were loved unconditionally by someone. Remember how it felt on either end of that love.

Unconditional love is the highest respect and acceptance that you can offer to another person and is a genuine and honest concern for their welfare. It is undemanding and without preconceptions and expectations. It is never to use the power of love to bargain with or withhold in order to hurt someone. Sometimes, it is loving someone enough to let them go or to stop helping them when we know that our help is stopping them from growing.

It is recognising your own and others' value and worth. It is keeping the channel of pure love open and allowing it to flow out towards whomever we meet. It is undoubtedly the most powerful resource that we have.

A person that loves unconditionally brings out the best in people and things. They will accept others as they are, seeing behind the layers that their personalities and belief systems may have put in the way. They will recognise the light within them and because of this, help to bring it forth.

They will seek the highest truth and will not be afraid to speak it but will be open to the fact that truth will constantly be unfolding itself to them in all sorts of ways.

They will be able to detach from their negative emotions; work through them and release them out of self-respect. They will accept the world as it is but expect it to be all that it can be, and so their world will be a friendly and loving place to live in. They will live in a world that loves them as much as they love it.

Here is a meditation so that you may tap into the resource of unconditional love:

Unconditional Love

Relax and deepen yourself ... Allow your mind to become still and quiet ... Let go of all the distractions of the day ... Gently drift into relaxation ...

Now imagine a column of rose pink light descending from the universe on to the top of your head ... It is the pure energy of Love ... Now open your mind to receiving this light ... imagine it entering your head, filling your brain and then spilling into your body ... Feel the light of Love fill your entire being, nourishing and regenerating every cell in your body ... It is freely and unconditionally given to you ... The Higher Power of the universe loves you simply because you exist ... because that is the nature of pure love ...

You have channeled the light of Unconditional Love into your being and now you can allow it to flow outwards ... Still remaining aware of the column of light entering your head from above, start to radiate the pink light from your heart centre (the middle of your chest) ... Direct it towards those dear to you ... towards those you feel any resistances in loving ... to those people you feel any animosity towards ... to those who have hurt you in some way ... Feel the light of Unconditional Love flowing outwards ... healing and empowering both you, the giver, and those that receive ...

See the Love transforming your life and positively influencing the world around you ... Send the light of Love into parts of the world that needs healing ...

Now wrap the Earth up in the pink of Love ... Hold it in Love until you wish to return your awareness back to your body ... Affirm that you will use the power of Unconditional Love in your everyday life ... and when you feel ready gently open your eyes ...

Repeat this as often as you wish to connect with the power of unconditional love.

To help to to bring more unconditional love into your life, try devoting a whole day (or week), when everyone you meet you silently greet with, "I see the light within you and love you unconditionally". Remind yourself throughout the day to look through all the outer trappings of a person and see the pure consciousness within them; in fact, someone just like yourself. The more you do this, the more the temptation to judge or criticise anyone will become less and less.

Unconditional love opens our heart centre. In the chakra (energy centre) system, the heart is in the centre. Very briefly, for those not familiar with this system, a chakra is a vortex of energy which acts as a doorway for vital energy to enter from the etheric to the physical body. Energy also flows outwards through the chakras from the physical back out to the etheric to create our reality. The chakras are located along the spine.

There are three lower chakras. The first (base) is concerned with security, bonding with parents and grounding to the earth, the second (sacral) is concerned with sexuality, pleasure and creativity and the third (solar plexus) being to do with individuality, intellect and where we store negative emotions.

The three higher chakras are the fifth (throat) which is communication, integration and loyalty, the sixth (brow) is intuition, sensitivity and imagination and the seventh is our link to our higher consciousness, idealism and selfless service.

Our heart centre is the gateway to the higher centres. It is the link between the physical and spiritual aspects of ourselves. When we make the choice to link with other people through the heart centre, the connections will have more emotional clarity and depth than connections made at the lower centres. In opening our hearts to love, we become more open to the qualities of compassion, forgiveness, understanding, peace and contentment. We open our hearts to love simply by choosing to receive it and allowing it to flow into our lives.

It is the power of unconditional love that will not only transform our own lives and immediate environments but also will ultimately transform our world.

Part Five: The Illusion of Separateness

26 The Collective Unconscious

The Collective Unconscious was a term given by Carl Jung to explain the deeper level of our unconscious that links the human family together. To illustrate the various levels of our consciousness, he gave the analogy of an iceberg. The visible part of the iceberg is our conscious minds, the two-thirds of the iceberg that is below the surface of the water is our unconscious minds and the sea bed on which the iceberg rests is the collective unconscious.

Jung said that the lessons learned by ancestors were deposited in the collective unconscious and inherited by later generations. This inheritance is not direct but rather it predisposes the individual to react in a particular way in certain situations. The collective unconscious is universal and, according to Jung, is the fundamental base for man's psyche.

A useful illustration of the way the collective unconscious (some call it the collective mind) works is the study that Japanese scientists made of a colony of monkeys on an island. The monkeys' favourite food was a kind of sweet potato. One day, they observed one of the monkeys washing his potatoes in the sea before eating it. Before long all the monkeys on the island followed suit. "Nothing special about that" you may say, "They simply copied him." However, the extraordinary thing was that five years later, monkeys on a neighbouring island also began to wash their potatoes before eating them. There was no physical link between the two islands.

Tapping into the collective unconscious can be a double edged sword, however. Through it we can tap into the genius of Van Gogh but also his madness. We can tap into the heroic determination of Emmeline Pankhurst but also her pain and frustration. It is all a part of us; every virtuous and loving gesture that has ever been offered since time began as well as every murderous and cruel impulse. It all exists on the level of the collective unconscious.

If ever we find ourselves judging or criticising another for their actions whatever they may be, we could look deep within us to find, at the level of the collective unconscious, the same emotions and causes to that action. This can give us understanding and compassion but it will take away the luxury of feeling superior or self-righteous. A small price to pay!

We are all linked, and awareness of this link gives us a responsibility for the human family. We do have impact; our thoughts, words and actions do have impact on the whole.

Fountain International utilises this collective phenomenon for healing communities. It is a totally non-sectarian, world-wide healing project. Local groups meet to meditate together in order to send healing energy to a focal point in their community. They also commit themselves to sending that energy at an agreed time each day.

It started in Brighton in 1981 and its name comes from the focal point they used – the fountain in The Old Steine. They visualised sending their healing energy to the fountain and then imagined it flowing out into the community. After a while they observed a decrease in street violence and the local council voted a "clean up Brighton" campaign. Results were also observed by dowsers who discovered that the energy fields associated with nearby ley-lines (lines of magnetic energy) had expanded.

We are all powerful healers in our own individual rights but when we combine our energies, we can heal the planet. This is what organisations such as Fountain International have as their aims. Group activity can produce a total that is greater than the sum of the parts.

I was once on a residential healing course held by Matthew Manning. On the fourth day, we formed a healing circle. We all held hands while Matthew went around the circle giving us each healing. He is a very powerful healer. It felt like a warm current of energy flowing through me when he had his hands on my shoulders. He encouraged us to imagine the healing energy flowing around the circle.

It was an incredible experience. At one stage, I felt my individual identity dissolve as I melted into what I can only describe as a ring of golden, shimmering consciousness which was the group. When this feeling partially subsided, I saw a vision of pink and gold angels hovering above the healing circle forming a dome above us.

Afterwards, I felt a little shy about sharing my vision with the group but the lady next to me said, "It was strange. I have never thought about angels before in my life but I saw them above us while we were doing that". I then told her I saw them too and there was a chorus of people saying that they had also seen the angels. Out of the group of forty people, there seemed to be half of them that had shared the same vision. Had we linked together on the collective unconscious? Had we all just imagined it? I don't really know, but I do know that it was an amazing experience that showed me not only how healing energy can be magnified within a group but also the magic of shared consciousness; how, when we dare to let down our boundaries of identity and persona, we can blend into one pure consciousness.

Because of the advances that technology is making, our lives are becoming more and more linked and interactive. Through the media we are very often tuning in to the same input at the same time. Whatever the negative considerations that we may have about this, it does not alter the fact that this is also bound to unify the collective mind. It is my hope that it fosters a collective sensitivity at the same time, but then that is really down to each and every one of us.

We have the choice as to what our individual contribution is to the collective unconscious. Are we going to pour in the pure energies of love, compassion and forgiveness or are we going to top it up with more negativity? Each time we allow love to flow into our lives and flow out through our actions in the world we are having a positive impact on the collective.

Love can be a state of mind where we are in total harmony with the life force of all living things. It is a state without judgement or criticism. It is a state of absolute peace that we can attain when we reach down deep within us to the stillness that is waiting there in each moment.

Also, each time we release any of our negative emotions such as fear, anger, resentment or hate we are also cleansing it from the collective unconscious. As we clear those dark corners of the collective psyche, we make more room for something more valid, more relevant to who we are to become. We make even more room for Love.

27 The Family of Humanity

Ram Dass once said, "Everywhere I look, I see God in drag". I love that expression because it looks beyond the personality, the body, all the judgements of 'better than' and 'worse than' to see the one consciousness that is common to us all. The one that goes even deeper than the collective unconscious; the consciousness that provided the spark to ignite our life.

Since my daughter, Rhianon, was a very young child she was able to express profound insights in a simple, concise way that so often would delight me with their wisdom. During her first week of infant's school, she returned home with her hands on her hips and that look on her face that told me she was deep in thought and said, "Mum, those kids at school are silly. They think that God sits on a cloud with a white cloak and long beard. That's not right is it? God is life, is everywhere, in everyone and everything we can see and feel". Well, what do you say to a five year old coming out with something like that? I probably said something pretty inane like, "Yes, dear. What would you like for tea?" but I did feel grateful for that little pearl of wisdom.

I sometimes think that our bodies are like spacesuits that we need to wear to become acclimatized to earth's conditions. They serve us pretty well, too. They need a little care and when they can no longer be maintained, we trade them in for new ones. But the body is not the only protective layer that we wear. We also wear our personality, our sense of identity, our psychological and emotional make-up, maybe our defences of fear and all the other issues that we have looked at during this book.

All these 'garments' are like layers of an onion, we peel one off and there is another, and another and so on until we reach the seed of pure consciousness, life force, the divine spark; whatever you wish to call it. It is at this core that we are all one. To be conscious of this oneness is not to lose our identity. Our identity is a vehicle to lead us to remember that oneness. Our unique path to that remembering will always remain unique.

There are those days, after I have been meditating on the oneness of all life, when I feel related to everyone I see. I have been in London for the day and it seems as if I recognise all the people that pass me in the street. It is such a wonderful feeling and I usually have great adventures on those days; meet fascinating people and see interesting things. I realise that those people and things would have been there anyway but I have opened up to receiving them in to my awareness.

We are related to the whole family of humanity. The illusion of separateness is the greatest illusion of all. We are all one family, one consciousness. The central theme of all the world's religions is the breaking through of this illusion to reach the knowledge of the interdependence of all life. This theme may have been distorted, hidden or undervalued in the dogmatisation of the religious institutions but it is still there. In fact the root meaning of the word 'religion' is to reconnect, to remember.

Try this meditation in order to remember that connection. You can do it with your partner, a friend or relative. You can even do it when you are on the Tube or bus, in the supermarket or garage. (If you do it with an unsuspecting stranger, you will need to be quite surreptitious!) It may also be beneficial to do this with a person you find difficult to love. Visualise them in from of you and do the meditation with them as if they were there with you.

Connecting Meditation

Look into your partner's eyes. Let yourself become aware of the energy within that person, the strength and endurance, the love and wisdom. Think of how those energies could help heal our planet. Allow yourself to feel a strong desire for this person to be free of suffering, greed and hatred for all of their life ...

Now become aware of that person's pain, the suffering, disappointments and failures that they have endured during their life. Share with them their pain and allow yourself to feel a deep compassion for them ... Feel the desire to lift their sorrow from them ...

Now drop your awareness to a place deep within you ... below your personality, your mind, your emotions, down to that pure consciousness. Breathe down into that place that connects you to this person as well as to the whole family of humanity. Be aware of the intricate web of relationship that is at the core of your being, that place where you are one with all life. Feel that peace and rest within it for a while. Reconnect and remember ...

When you feel ready, bring your awareness back to the room and gently open your eyes ...

A termitary is like a single animal whose organs, muscles and bones have not fused together. The queen ant is the brain and each section of the community has specific functions in the organism of the community. Everything is exceedingly well-regulated and geared to the benefit of the whole.

The family of humanity has similarities with the termitary in that each member constitutes an integral part of the whole. However, the termite has a blind, unconscious programme to fulfil and that is where we differ so much from the ants. We have the gift (some may say curse!) of free will. The free will to go from one extreme to another; to isolate ourselves from others and follow the course of our own lives without much concern for anyone else or to live a life of service to others without due regard for ourselves. But hopefully we can manage to find that fine balance between the awareness of our individuality and that of our interdependence with all living things.

Individual consciousness can bring peace of mind but there may be the danger of isolation or an ego trip into self-importance. Self-love may become self-serving. This can happen when individual consciousness does not follow its natural course into a consciousness of our interdependence.

However, on the other end of the scale, if we do not assume personal responsibility for our lives, we may be tempted to give our power away to the collective. By this I mean identifying ourselves with a group, political party, religion or sect to the point of losing our sense of self. There have always been those charismatic individuals that manipulate people on this level. There are religious sects that seek to strip the devotee of their individuality, their personal history. Some of the methods have been likened to those used for brainwashing. There have been tragic incidents of mass suicides instigated by leaders of such cults.

Remember John Lennon's inspiring song "Imagine"? "Imagine there's no countries, no religions too." What a thought, not anarchy or an unholy state of decadence without the guidance of established religions, but one in which each human being takes responsibility for themselves **and** their integral part within the human family.

When we choose to be an active member of the family of humanity we go from demanding rights to reassuming our essential part as a human being. We voluntarily surrender to the good of the whole from our love of the whole. We raise ourselves above our instinctive levels of survival and fear's domain and into the realm of pure consciousness. In this realm all that exists is the creative energy of love, nothing more, nothing less.

28 The Lessons of Separateness

I am going to take the liberty of starting this chapter with a story that we can use as a model to uncover the lessons of separateness. It is a model which gives meaning to me but please just let it rumble around in your mind for a while and see if it resonates with you. If it doesn't, just read it as if it were a fairy story.

Emerging from the Source of all life, the male and female energies of the Universe, the God and the Goddess, entwined in a loving embrace and began to dance. From this beautiful, cosmic dance a child was born. The child was born in love and was love, a shimmering light body of pure consciousness at one with the Source, with the God and the Goddess.

The child desired to know more about itself. As this desire increased, the various dimensions of the child separated, differentiated until they became conscious of their individuality. This process continued until the child had separated each cell of its body into separate life forms, each aware of its uniqueness as well as its connection to the whole body.

The cells of the body took on denser forms and the density created the illusion of separateness. Each separate cell developed individual consciousness with the consciousness of the whole body held deep within. They learned, through the diversity of form, the dance of creation. The great adventure had begun.

The adventure takes them through the learning experiences that their physical separateness entails including a forgetfulness of the reality of their unity, the pain of separation, the joy of playing with each other and the discovery of loving connections through that play. It leads them to the outer limits of the illusion of separation until a deep longing within them urges them to remember the source of their lives; remember that the human family is one body, one consciousness. At this point, they begin the journey back to oneness.

The journey is an inner one. By looking deep within to find the pure consciousness that is one with all life, the direction is found. Those that choose the journey become map-makers for others. Those others will not follow blindly but will be inspired to find and tread their own unique path.

The Child will become one again. Its disparate parts will come together voluntarily and joyfully, each fulfilling their unique function in the body of the Child. No function will be considered greater or lesser, more or less important or integral. Then the Child will have the full consciousness to be able to reunite with its parents, the God and Goddess, and ultimately the Source.

In the human fetus, we do not know why one particular cell ultimately manifests as a heart, another a muscle or yet another as a bone. We also do not understand the differentiation and individuation of human beings. We label and classify people according to class, colour, race, job, psychological type, astrological sign, yet do not know why one person will function in one role of life rather than another. We are free to express our uniqueness in isolation or to identify ourselves with a country, religion or political party or in a wider context of humanity itself and the pure consciousness that binds it together.

However, we can observe the results of the varying modes of expression not only on the individual but on society as a whole. Isolation brings with it the pain and emptiness of loneliness. Aligning our energies with collective groups may rob us of our right to question and search for meaning within ourselves. However, denying our universal interconnectedness by narrowing the awareness of the collective (for instance, fundamentalism, nationalism, fanaticism) causes rifts between nations and builds barriers between people. In searching for the meaning of our lives, we also seek balance between our collectivity and individuality.

So what can we learn from the illusion of separateness? It can lead us to discover the joy of exploration, to learn how to play, to remember, how to use the physical body as a wonderful vehicle to enjoy the adventure. From separateness, we return to the consciousness of oneness with the full knowledge of the pain of separation. We understand that all the pain we suffer in isolation is a longing, a yearning to return to Spirit. We learn that we are the creators of our reality, our distortions and truths. We can create heaven or hell for ourselves; it is our choice. We learn how to use defences such as victimhood, matyrdom and blame while we are growing and how to cast them off when they are not necessary.

We learn that we can choose to love and be loved, to allow the pure energy of love to flow through us and remind us of who we really are.

29 Visions of The Future

I have always been an optimist. I remember startling a couple of Jehovah's Witnesses once with my optimism. The first thing they said when I opened the door was, "Do you feel there is any hope for this world?" They had a dour expression on their face (mind you I guess **anyone** would if they had spent all day having doors slammed in their face) and they seemed to expect me to say that I felt no hope and fully expected the world to end imminently. Instead I spoke of how I see the proof of my belief in a positive future for humanity all around me.

Although we have polluted the earth and its atmosphere, there is also a growing sense of responsibility especially amongst the children who are, after all, our future. Children are very often acting as their parents' conscience, urging them to buy biodegradable products, saving energy and reducing waste. They are involved in so many environmental projects at their schools it encourages us adults to look more closely at our lifestyles.

Then there are the environmental groups themselves, educating people and campaigning for a cleaner world. They show us practical steps we can each take in order to make a positive difference through our individual actions. They campaign and influence public opinion to persuade the politicians of the world and industry to take action.

There are self-help groups setting up all over the place. Communities of people helping and supporting each other with similar problems. They are made up of people taking responsibility for themselves and as a result caring for others that have gone through or are going through the same issues.

All these things give me hope and inspiration. Sometimes it is so hard to read the newspapers and watch the news on the radio and maintain a sense of balance. The media will only give you the news on the 'bad guys', the devastation, the declines, etc. You will not be kept fully informed of the progress of the growing movement of people that are working for the environment, that are working toward world peace, that are caring for the homeless, sick and lonely but there are countless people working quietly behind the scenes as well as in the forefront of public affairs.

'World Goodwill Newsletter' is a free quarterly bulletin which gives information on world affairs with details of the work and programme of World Goodwill. This is a non-governmental organisation of the United Nations and devoted to the promotion of World Goodwill. This newsletter gives in-depth articles on the movement toward world peace and harmony such as the conference in Chicago last year of all the major world religions where they discussed their similarities rather that their differences. Another issue may be devoted to the global problem of drugs and will set out the United Nations' global programme of action against drug abuse. For me, reading this bulletin and other alternative magazines that give us the 'other news', gives me a balance between, on the one side, the horror and tragedy that is present in our world and on the other, the compassion, integrity and determination of the human spirit.

There certainly is a powerful movement afoot and it is generated by each one of us doing the best we can in our own individual lives, cleansing our own hearts of hatred and anger, healing our emotions and releasing the past. The deep desires of each person form a dynamic force. We have witnessed the collective desire of individual people pulling the Berlin Wall down and ending the Cold War. It has virtually ended hostilities in Northern Ireland and back in the '60s, it ended the bloody war in Vietnam.

Our world is a wonderful school. We may have some difficult lessons to learn but we can ask for help from our fellow pupils and help them in return with theirs. We will find many teachers and they may appear in the most unlikely forms or places but if we remain open and receptive, we will complete the curriculum.

If we keep the classroom tidy and treat it with respect, it will be a while yet before the school bell rings and school's out.

In this book, we have looked at so many ways in which we can heal our lives and create a positive and loving future. We have looked at how to manifest a beautiful reality by clearing out the negative beliefs that hinder it, visualising it and then allowing it to become manifest. Imagination, desire and expectation are the tools with which we can create our reality. It is the same for our world.

We need to develop a vision, not only for ourselves but for the world. We can each envisage a world transformed and, if that vision is backed up with desire and expectation, we can manifest it. Think about what kind of a world you desire and what you expect. Is there a difference? What kind of a world can you envisage? Start here, with the vision. Allow your imagination to take flight and show you a vision of a glorious future.

This will awaken the desire and the expectation of a wonderful reality filled with love, fun and laughter. Our imagination will provide the spark to light the dream we hold deep within us. The dream we may have buried long ago when we forgot our connection to each other and when we forgot that at the core of our being, there is only love.

When we awaken the dream within us, whatever action we take or abstain from will be of love. Within the dream is the solution to all the world's sorrows and ailments. So let us dare to dream.

Useful addresses

Alcoholics Anonymous
PO Box 1
Stonebow House
Stonebow
York
Y01 2NJ

Fountain International
PO Box 52
Torquay
Devon
TQ2 8PE

The National College of Hypnosis and Psychotherapy
12 Cross Street,
Nelson,
Lancashire
BB9 7EN

For a list of Ram Dass tapes:
The Open Gate
1 Woodman's Cottage
Brocham End
Bath
BA1 9BZ

For tapes and books by Lazaris:
The New Magick Co
Southcroft
Burhill Park
Burwood Road
Walton-on-Thames
Surrey
KT12 4BE

For tapes, books by Lazaris and workshop information,
Concept Synergy
302 South County Road
Suite 109
Palm Beach
FL 33480-4245
USA

Angel Cards from:
Phoenix Mail Order
The Park
Forres
Scotland
IV36 OTZ

World Goodwill Newsletter
3 Whitehall Court
Suite 54
LONDON
SW1A 2EF

World Goodwill
113 University Place
11th Floor
PO Box 722
Cooper Station
New York
NY 10276
USA

For tapes by Sue Vaughan write for brochure to:
Aurora Cassettes
12 Springfield Road
WINDSOR
Berkshire
SL4 3PQ

In the U.S.A.
The Light Institute of Galisteo
Rt.3, Box 50
Galisteo
NM 87540

For information on workshops,
Shakti Gawain
PO Box 377

Mill Valley
CA 94942
USA

Tapes and books by Shakti Gawain,
Nataraj Publishing
PO Box 2627
Mill Valley
CA 949442
USA

Bibliography

Andrews L, The Power Deck, Harper Collins, New York, 1991.

Bach R, Jonathan Livingston Seagull, Pan Books, London, 1973.

Cappacchione L, The Power of Your Other Hand, Newcastle Pub, 1988.

Cousins N, Anatomy of an Illness as Perceived by the Patient, Bantam Books, 1981.

Emmanuel's Book, Compiled by Pat Rodegast & Judith Stanton, Bantam, 1987.

Fordham F, An Introduction to Jung's Psychology, Penguin Books, England, 1986.

Gawain S, Living in the Light, Eden Grove, London, 1988.

Hay L L, You Can Heal Your Life, Eden Grove, London, 1988.

Hodgson-Burnett F, The Secret Garden, Michael Joseph, London, 1986.

Jung C, Collected Works, vol 9, Princetown University Press, 1953.

Lerner & Lerner, The Inner Child Cards, Bear & Co, Sante Fe, 1992.

Sams & Carson, Medicine Cards, Bear & Co, Sante Fe, 1988.